MUST HISTORY REPEAT ITSELF?

MUST HISTORY REPEAT ITSELF?

A study of the lessons taught by the (repeated) failure and (occasional) success of government economic policy through the ages

ANTONY FISHER

PUBLISHED BY CHURCHILL PRESS LIMITED

2 Cecil Court London Road Enfield Middlesex

1974

First published in 1974 by
CHURCHILL PRESS LIMITED
© A.G.A. Fisher 1974

Printed and bound by
Tonbridge Printers Limited
Tonbridge, Kent

CONTENTS

BIOGRAPHICAL NOTE

Antony Fisher was born in London in 1915, educated at Eton and Cambridge, served in the RAF as a Battle of Britain pilot and was awarded the AFC.

After a period in the City he became a full-time farmer in Sussex, learned of the broiler industry during a lecture tour in the USA, and in 1954 established the pioneering Buxted Chicken Company (later merged into Allied Farm Foods) which succeeded without government subsidy or protection in making record profits and dramatically reducing the price of chicken to the consumer. Mr Fisher was a leading critic of the theory and practice of the British Egg Marketing Board from 1956 until it was wound up in January 1969.

In 1955 Mr Fisher founded the Institute of Economic Affairs as an independent research and educational trust of which he is chairman of the Trustees. In 1970 he established the International Institute of Economic Research on a similar pattern. He has lectured extensively in the USA and elsewhere on contemporary economic questions.

He divides his time between London and Sussex where he owns a dairy herd of 500 cows and manages a similar number for independent farmers. He is a founder director of Mariculture Ltd., the first commercial enterprise concerned with breeding turtles in the Grand Cayman Island, where he is also developing a dairy herd.

FOREWORD

GRAHAM HUTTON

An honourable fate attends the farsighted few: they sow old truths with unpalatable seeds; they reap ridicule and obloquy. Of such were Adam Smith, Cobden and Bright in their time; Orwell and Hayek in ours. Ridicule and contempt were always expressed in terms like 'Oh, but what you recommend is politically impossible!' Sooner rather than later, however, the politically impossible occurred. Those who, incredulous, read *The Road to Serfdom* in the last year of the last war, and *1984* in the first years of the so-called peace, know that what looked politically impossible *then* is happening *now*. For Orwell's and Hayek's memorials, we have only to look around in Britain—and beyond.

Mr Anthony Fisher is a remarkable, that is to say a noteworthy, man. He writes what he believes, and what he believes he has derived from much practical experience as well as study. His practical experience proved for him extremely profitable when many foretold failure in a field of rural enterprise which was utterly unsubsidised. He has written this book from a deep conviction that our feet in Britain have been set by all manner of governments since 1945 on a slippery, though primrose, path. As an on-the-whole decent, honest, incorrupt, taxpaying people we have for nearly three decades suffered from a damnably dangerous consensus, leading all governments to hamstring our individual economic energy and our collective discipline of enterprise. The hamstrings, without which we

vii

limp and lag behind others, are slashed by levies, restricting the expression of choice, the exertion of enterprise, and the thrust of self-help or self-improvement.

Hardly anyone would gainsay that as a people we have steadily lagged in economic improvement behind our nearest neighbours, and even behind some farther off like Japan and Spain. To ensure 'full employment' by guaranteeing every worker his old and loss-making job, and every concern its long-established output, at the taxpayers' expense is not what Keynes and Lloyd George meant when they proclaimed *We Can Conquer Unemployment* four decades ago. But that is what we go on doing by more and more nationalisation of older trades and industries, more and more state or local government levies upon people to secure narrower and worse choices—if any at all.

Mr Fisher amply shows how and why our friends and neighbours have done, and do, better. Few in Britain realise that in 'the socialist paradise' of Sweden the state has not taken over anything like the percentage of the economy that Britain under all governments has now reached. That Germany, France, Switzerland, the United States, Canada, Holland, Belgium, Italy and others superficially like us at present experience inflation, as we do, is no rebuttal of Mr Fisher's argument since inflation is contagious. It remains true that we go on lagging behind all of them in economic performance.

Nor is that all. In an era of catchwords tossed around by what I term the 'consensus intelligentsia' of the media of public communication, we are over-treated to slogan-bashing like 'the environment' or 'the quality of life', whereby we are invited to believe that our way of not-producing, not-working, not-economising and not-profiting is better than that of other men. Meanwhile the same pundits and their opponents complain that our poor are 'getting poorer' (which is factually untrue, they are getting better-off *more slowly* than all other Britons); that our state services (from telephones and mail to fuel and rail) are disgracefully bad; that our National Health Service is deteriorating in comparison not only with that of other countries but also with what it was; that our public education system is split between totalitarian stereotypists and those they prevent from raising (or maintaining) standards of performance; that all public authorities' so-called services cost more, become under-manned, and get worse; and finally, that our money loses half its purchasing power every seven years now, as contrasted with every twenty years only a decade ago.

It is a pretty formidable indictment. But it is fair comment. And it is in damning contrast to what has gone on, is going on, in other countries near and like us.

There is worse to follow. The same consensus intelligentsia invites us to believe that it can all be put right by more and more of the same policies that have caused the malaise. Mr Fisher does not believe that. Nor do I. On the contrary, he believes—and from close analysis of facts and figures he reasonably argues—that those of us capable of independent thought ought to be radically re-examining these past 28 years of so-called economic and social re-organisation in Britain. He believes we are actually travelling the wrong path; not that we can somehow wriggle through to better days by the old ways. He believes we must radically set free all the economic limbs of the country and all the economic energies of individuals to work for the betterment of the country through betterment of their own and their families' lot. It is no new argument: Adam Smith expounded it; West Germany, Japan, Belgium, France, Italy, Hong Kong, Indonesia and many others have applied and are applying it. We are not. They are not hamstrung in their progress. We are.

This book comes most aptly upon its hour. Many Britons today have an uneasy sense of sands running out. Mr Fisher's argument from experience and history, his case for enlarging rather than narrowing freedoms of enterprise, and his call for choice, self-help and self-improvement are required reading for the politically-minded. The consensus intelligentsia will say, as ever, that his prescription is 'politically impossible'. That has been so often said and so often proved wrong. If this time it proves true, so much the worse for all of us.

But it is right that he should say these things in Britain today, and that they should be reasonably discussed by reasoning people. So I commend his book for honesty of purpose and integrity of reasoning to all who want 'a better Britain' in both material and non-material ways, and who wish to know what should be done to set us on the right path.

October 1973   GRAHAM HUTTON

INTRODUCTION

Even the most cursory study of the history of the human race provides evidence of constant human failure, leading to violence and man's inhumanity to man. Those who have lived through the most recent expressions of this violence—the Second World War, the wars in Korea and in Vietnam, the Castro Revolution, the Russian invasions of Hungary and Czechoslovakia, and the Chinese purges—will know something of the stress, the pain, the fear and the hysteria that such devastating explosions produce in man.

On the Sunday nearest to 11 November each year memorial services to the dead of the two great wars are held in many countries. But these memorial services, together with the many statues and plaques dedicated 'in lasting memory' to those who have given their lives, regrettably do little or nothing to prevent similar ghastly events in the future. Memories, and even memorials, fade as the unsolved problems of the past simply take on slightly new forms.

Back to first principles

As I relate in the pages that follow, there is sufficient similarity between unhappy developments in history to challenge our intellectual abilities to explain what keeps going wrong. This book is my effort to meet that challenge.

In Chapter 1, I study three possible explanations of why things go wrong. The first is that everything which happens is a matter of random chance. Existence itself would then be no more than the spinning of an infinite number of roulette wheels supported by an infinite number of games. But as Einstein once wrote: 'I cannot believe that God plays dice with the world'.

A second possibility is that on countless occasions throughout history a few evil men have acquired the understanding and power to trick the vast majority of mankind into conditions of misery or slavery using coercion, revolution and even war to that end.

A third possibility is that some natural order exists in the form of an infinite variety of cause-and-effect relationships, but that we do not yet understand them sufficiently to run our affairs harmoniously. It would follow that the economic and social disasters which continually overwhelm us come about, not only because we are unaware of these relationships but also because we are almost certainly unaware that any such principles could exist. If this latter proposition is true, it is possible to make sense of man's recurring disasters. History and modern experience would then fit into place and point inexorably to further periods of misery and chaos unless cause and effect are correctly understood and applied.

In Chapter 2, therefore, I go on to offer a more detailed study of cause-and-effect relationships, explaining how man's troubles could have arisen because he himself has been ignorant of their existence. One major problem is that, like the principle of gravity, the many forces acting on each of us as individuals are invisible and intangible while only the consequences are discernible to man's physical senses. I then try to show how the understanding of cause-and-effect relationships can have tremendous consequences. Quite contrary to general opinion, the politician whose duty it is to create new laws or change old laws is seldom, if ever, an originator. Nor are the communications media usually the prime mover. Neither the politician nor the journalist has time enough for thought or research, and both inevitably become immersed in compromise and short-term calculations. I give reasons for thinking that new understanding has to come from independent ind- ividuals who can give sufficient time to intellectual study.

Letting history speak

Chapter 3 dips into history over a period of almost five thousand years. There is much evidence that wars, started for various reasons, regularly result in the creation of bureaucracies and taxes. When the wars are over, the bureaucracies and the taxes increase rather than decrease, which in turn creates inflationary conditions. Again and again governments then attempt to hold down wages and prices by law without solving the problem.

History also provides evidence that where govern- ments have pursued the opposite policy of maximising individual choice within a framework of law and moral conduct, their problems have given way to prosperity. Hence my conviction that history does teach lessons, provided that the past experience of mankind can be studied in the light of what I call cause-and-effect relationships or others may describe as principles.

I owe an explanation to the reader for the many quotations particularly in Chapter 3. Because I am not an historian, I have thought it more appropriate to rely on original quotations which I believe give the argument more strength than I could give it in my own words.

In Chapter 4, I apply the same basic thinking to more recent experience. Examples are drawn from agriculture both within the United Kingdom and elsewhere, and from industry and commerce throughout the world, to illustrate that success or failure of govern- ment policies does depend on the application of right principles. In Chapter 5, I produce evidence for my conviction that theoretical study does yield practical consequences. I offer examples from my own experience that documented understanding, even by one person, can suffice to move government to make correct policy decisions. The essential ingredient is deep understanding, which in turn can be achieved only by dedicated concentration and research.

Chapter 6 is my attempt to document the final stage in this chain of thinking by setting out actions which the government must take to produce the benefits that have been sought by many and have evaded all. Among the consequences of policies deliberately planned to maximise individual choice will be low taxation and a maximum increase in the wealth of the poorer members of the community.

In this way I put my own theories to the test. I believe that it is hardly possible to say or write anything that has not been said or written before. But what I have written may be written in a way that is new. I have tried to unite the various arguments and contentions in a continuous whole leading to clear conclusions which have been incorporated in what politicians might call a manifesto. If I am right it will have inevitable consequences, possibly more quickly than anybody dare hope.

A personal note

My father was killed in the First World War in 1917. My only brother Basil was killed flying a Hurricane in the Battle of Britain on 15 August, 1940. He, our common friend David Berry, and I were members of 111 Hurricane Squadron. David Berry, for whom I had great respect, was killed flying his Hurricane over

France even before the Battle of Britain commenced. I survived but with no thanks to my own efforts, for it was some time before I was to learn that the main ability for which I and my Squadron existed, to destroy enemy aircraft, was an ability I did not possess. Unaware of my inability, and maybe with a less than average inclination for violent aggression, I was no credit in that particular occupation.

Later I was to learn the great difficulty, even with eight machine-guns, of hitting an enemy plane. Yet as soon as I became aware of that difficulty, I became a more useful Royal Air Force officer. That tale is not for telling here; the point I wish to underline is that only when I became aware of an inability was I able to set about correcting it. From that moment I hope I became an asset and no longer a liability. I discovered that I was not the only fighter pilot who had been unaware of the great difficulty of hitting an enemy plane, or of the need for technical and strategic efficiency to fulfil the purpose a fighter pilot was expected to achieve. I learned that good intentions were not enough.

In the pages that follow I offer evidence which has convinced me that mankind is in much the same position as I was as an ignorant fighter pilot and in worse danger for being unaware of the need to correct that ignorance.

It must be true that any successful effort to achieve better understanding of the motives and behaviour of communities is a more enduring memorial to those who gave their lives for peace than any memorial in stone. Many have tried to add another rung to man's ladder of understanding. I offer the following pages as my own endeavour.

ACKNOWLEDGEMENTS

This book grew out of my efforts over more than a decade to compile evidence to show the difference between what I have more and more come to see as the right and wrong approaches of governments through the ages to 'solve' economic and social problems. From extensive reading, discussion, travel and varied business experience, I found no difficulty in assembling many historical examples, quotations, and experiences. Indeed, the growing bulk became so large that it was doubtful whether it could all go into one book.

What decided me to stop writing and start looking for a publisher was the almost uncanny way events began to bear out the warnings I have for years been making privately as a result of this study of history. Since 1970 Britain has drifted closer towards disaster under a Conservative Government which has failed, no less than its Labour predecessor, to apply the lessons taught by the past. Lacking experience in authorship, I therefore appealed to John Wood and Dr Rhodes Boyson for help in severely reducing to a manageable length a bulky manuscript that had 'just growed' like Topsy over more than ten years. After major surgery on the text, Ralph Harris undertook the difficult task of refining it into a form suitable for publication. For these three friends I have the greatest respect and warmest gratitude, as also for Graham Hutton who wrote the Foreword.

From many others to whom I am indebted for assistance at various stages, I must single out Sudha Shenoy who helped in research and checking and Joy Northey, my secretary for many years, who has typed and retyped material running to a length many times greater than appears here.

There are many colleagues in my business ventures and personal friends in America as well as England who have taught me much that I try to apply in this book. But above all I must express my debt to Professor F. A. Hayek who inspired my original interest in economic research almost 30 years ago and who has ever since encouraged me by his example and teachings to hold firm to the faith that it is the battle of ideas which will decide the future prospects of a free society.

A.G.A.F.

Dedicated to my brother, Basil

'They shall grow not old, as we that are left grow old;
Age shall not weary them, nor the years condemn.
At the going down of the sun and in the morning
We will remember them.'

LAURENCE BINYON

CHAPTER 1

Think it Out

THE ROLE OF PRINCIPLES

As we move into the mid-70s, people in the West are richer than they have ever been before—and this is probably also true of the people of the East. Despite the increase in material wealth since the last war, the process looks increasingly precarious. This book is written in the belief that history is about to repeat itself in the sense that future developments will not be all progress and may be downhill. My argument will be that economic progress stems from an appropriate form of government and that, more recently, growth has been despite—and not because of—our present form of government.

Familiar symptoms
Are we not trying to grapple with something which might be likened to a disease? Some politicians and journalists argue that what is happening is 'progress'. But that should lead to prosperity, happiness and a better life, whereas the trends that worry me point in the opposite direction. The following is a grim list of clearly discernible and recurring ingredients of the syndrome which threatens us:
  (a) a steady decrease in the freedom of choice available to the individual;
  (b) a steady increase in taxes;
  (c) a steady increase in the number of central and local civil servants;

(d) an extension of state ownership, often called 'nationalisation', done sometimes to 'help' firms and industries out of trouble;

(e) an accelerating decrease in the value of money, resulting in a continuing increase in prices;

(f) an increasing resistance to taxation in various forms of evasion;

(g) increasing discontent expressed particularly in industrial action, student unrest and civil disobedience;

(h) the fixing of wages and prices;

(i) a growing 'black market' in wages and the use of money;

(j) a tendency to ascribe any apparent benefits to state action, and to blame difficulties on individuals as 'strikers', 'profiteers', 'landlords', 'speculators';

(k) a weakening of the rule of law and the protection of the individual by the state, which curtails rather than preserves personal rights;

(l) a steady deterioration in moral standards.

These attacks on the individual, which can ultimately reduce his choice to zero, reflect political attempts to blame others for the failure of particular policies. If I am right, and if standards of living appear to be rising while the syndrome is developing, any improvement comes about *despite* government interference with the economy and not because of it.

As we will see, history provides much evidence that as the economic disease progresses, a familiar result has been the establishment of tyranny or dictatorship, when the state and its public functionaries become all-powerful. Government becomes a Frankenstein's Monster, 'a thing which gets out of the control of its creator'.

During recent centuries, one of the main objects of government has been to prevent any private individual or group obtaining too much power but, unless strong checks are established, there is a natural temptation for government to end up taking too much power for itself.

Since increasing government power reduces individual freedom, a point is reached when people feel driven to resist, even at the risk of disorder and sometimes revolution.

The source of wealth

Some civilisations have been more successful than others, but there have been fewer periods of progress than of stagnation, retrogression and destruction. Such ebbing and flowing in the tides of human civilisation have been caused less by the vagaries of nature than by decisions made by men themselves.

It may seem obvious that the wealth of nations which are relatively rich and provide wider choices for their citizens, has come about because they owned abundant natural resources. Yet both China and Russia own tremendous quantities of valuable assets in the form of land and minerals but are pathetically poor compared with the USA or most European nations. The Venetians built up an empire without any resources and, indeed, probably developed their trading ability *because* they had no other resources. The Swiss have one of the strongest currencies in the world, but it is not backed by physical resources. Hong Kong, in recent years, has also shown itself a remarkable creator of wealth under the most unlikely circumstances. A rock without even a water supply has become first a trading centre and then a manufacturing challenger to better-endowed nations.

It is plain that the wealth of nations develops from other factors than merely the natural resources available. It may even be argued that physical advantages remove the competitive necessity of having to take thought and action, which in turn stimulates the mind and body to great achievements.

Do we need theory?

Economics is the study of man's decision-making in the use of scarce resources. Although it governs a large part of human action, its study is apt to bewilder people, if it does not frighten them off.

If we wish to build houses, we study architecture. If we wish to build bridges or power stations, we study engineering and physics. If we wish to fly to the moon, we have to study many sciences, including physics, chemistry and advanced mathematics. In such activities, the experts can agree sufficiently to avoid frequent failure. Yet when we consult economists, we find they disagree on almost every practical issue. My case here is that unless we can understand the central principles of economics the practical consequences will become increasingly unpleasant.

Although governments are nowadays guided by 'economists', they are as wanderers in a desert without a compass, without knowledge of the stars, without maps, or, worse still, with faulty instruments and inaccurate maps. The more surely human beings have been able to establish given relationships between cause and consequence in mathematics, physics and chemistry, the more surely have veritable miracles of scientific progress been achieved. The study of economics has certainly lagged far behind.

Newton and Einstein

Not surprisingly, successful businessmen often scorn economists and go on to doubt the value of any kind of economic theory. Yet, as in the physical sciences, correct theory must come before effective action. Of course, theories can be right or wrong and will have corresponding consequences. The problem is not whether to employ theory, but how to distinguish good from bad theories.

Newton was the first to discover and relate the laws of gravity and motion in such a way that theory became a practical guide to action so that the relationship between cause and effect could be used to achieve predictable results. It would have been impossible to land men on the moon and return them to earth without first understanding a great deal of theory.

One big difficulty in understanding theories about economic forces is that they are intangible. To understand them it is necessary to use our mental capacity and for this reason these forces seem quite unreal to many people. Nevertheless they are extraordinarily powerful and sure achievement depends on our precise understanding of them. Deciding economic policy without discovery of the correct theory is action without thought, which is not only wasteful but dangerous.

Even where politicians or their advisers do give time to thinking, their final policies have increasingly come to be based on a large measure of compromise or consensus, that is, on a mixture of true and false theories. Imagine trying to land men on the moon by a compromise of conflicting theories!

In order to simplify the discussion, I shall use the word 'principle' to refer to a basic assumption or a relationship between a cause and its effect.[1] In trying to study the consequences and the causes of government action, I am searching for economic principles which will achieve the desired ends in the most effective way. It is important not to confuse man-made laws with natural laws, such as gravity, which will function and produce their consequences whatever man may or may not know and think about them. Since man-made laws do not assume there are principles on which legislation should be based, it is not surprising they produce disturbing, if not disastrous consequences despite well-intentioned and desirable aims.

One classic example of the power and consequences of the understanding of correct theory is that of Einstein, who once worked in the Swiss Patent Office. His perception of physics and mathematics was such that he was able theoretically to work out a formula which is expressed as $E=MC^2$ and which has revolutionised our sources of energy. Today no military leader can disregard the consequences that have arisen from Einstein's understanding of powerful forces. Einstein's theories are very 'practical' in that they have had physical consequences which can be predetermined and created at will. In 1938 Einstein wrote a letter to President Roosevelt suggesting that he investigate the possibility of producing an atom bomb. That letter made it impossible for either the Germans or the

[1] Dictionary definitions of the word 'principle' are: 'A basic truth, general law of cause and effect' (*Advanced Learners' Oxford Dictionary*). 'A law of nature by virtue of which a given mechanism etc. brings about certain results . . . a comprehensive truth or proposition from which others are derived . . . general truth forming a basis for reasoning or action . . . fundamental cause' (*Cassell*). 'A primary element, force or law which produces or determines particular results' (*Webster*).

Japanese to win the war. How potent can be the power of understanding of only one man!

Six ways of deciding
Some readers will no doubt be thinking that theory and principles may have their place in the physical world but that they cannot apply to man's activities. One assumption is that economics is a consequence of human decision-making which is itself unpredictable. It may appear reasonable to assume that since the individual is free to make up his mind, and since therefore he has wide choice in what actions he may take, there can be no pre-determined relationship between economic cause and economic consequence. The purpose of this study of theory, history and modern experience is to give reasons for thinking there is such a relationship. If there is and we can discover it, we can avoid the mistakes made in the past. If there is no such relationship, our trials and tribulations have come about by chance and not from any particular cause which might be avoided in the future—a dismal prospect indeed.

I am a layman and have not studied economics at college or university. What I have learnt, if it be anything at all, is from personal study and discussions with many economists. If economics is about the use of scarce resources, it must study human decision-making. Every decision must be motivated by the intention to produce a desired consequence. There would appear to be some six main methods of making decisions. These are in ascending order of reliability: superstition, wrong assumption, guessing, experiment, experience, and finally the scientific method when a known cause-and-effect relationship is completely understood. It is also true that decisions can be guided by instinct, emotion, dogma, and religion, but I consider each of these may fit into the six main categories, or are substitutes for conscious decision-making. Let us look at the main methods by which human beings make their decisions, starting with the most effective, namely the scientific method.

The *Oxford Dictionary* defines 'science' in part as

> 'a branch of study which is concerned either with a connected body of demonstrated truths or with observed facts systematically classified and more or less collated by being brought under general laws and which includes trustworthy methods of the discovery of new truths within its own domain.'

The study of physics can therefore be described as a science and the law of gravity as one of the principles on which this science is based. Scientific understanding can be applied to many decisions to achieve sure results, but for most decision-making science is not available and we have to use other methods. The next method most likely to provide sure results is experience. For some things that we do, we have learned from experience or have been taught by others how best to achieve them. The lessons of experience have to be adapted to changing circumstances but, where we have appropriate experience, the element of chance in the achievement of our aims is reduced. Education in school is partly an attempt by society to help the coming generations benefit from past experience.

But if neither science nor experience are available, the next most economical method for achieving a given end is experimentation. An experiment can be designed to test various methods and to find out which produces the desired consequences at the lowest cost. To experiment can be expensive where there are many alternative hypotheses to test, but often it is the cheapest method available. Much human effort is expended in the form of experimentation and often there is no other way.

Thus we have three more or less rational methods for making decisions. Experiment and experience are less effective than scientific theory but have to be used when it is not available. If none of these rational methods is possible, we are left with guessing or superstition which may be dignified with the description of 'wrong assumption'. The guessing process may be bolstered by dogma, fashion, instinct or emotion but the chance of success is nothing like 50:50 where there may be dozens or hundreds of alternative wrong decisions and only a single right one.

The least satisfactory methods of all for achieving decision-making must be superstition or wrong assumption. If guessing is hazardous with little chance of producing the right answer, superstition is even more certain to produce the wrong answers. History is full of examples of decisions made for superstitious reasons. Endlessly, Roman Emperors and Roman Generals and lesser folk relied on a 'religion' which was based on superstition. Millions of animals and humans must have been sacrificed over the centuries in this wasteful effort.

Where Marx was wrong . . .
As an example of an influential principle, let us examine Karl Marx's basic assumption that work creates wealth.

> 'A use value or useful article therefore has value because human labour in the abstract has been

embodied or materialised in it . . . How then is
the magnitude of this value to be measured?
Plainly, by the quantity of the value-creating
substance of the labour contained in the article.
The quantity of labour, however, is measured by
its duration, and labour-time in its turn finds its
standards in weeks, days and years . . . We see
then that that which determines the magnitude
of the value of any article is the amount of
labour socially necessary or the labour-time
socially necessary for its production.'[1]

Marx thus argued that the real value of anything is
made up of the labour time put into it. In the passages
quoted he used the words 'socially necessary' because
he realised that the exchange values of two articles
may be quite different from their respective costs.
Nevertheless, since his conclusions would break down
completely if he could not prove that wealth is always
necessarily created by work, he adopted the labour
theory of value. If wealth is always created by work,
and if the owner of a factory such as a shareholder
does no work, he must be stealing from the workers
when he takes profits. I am concerned here to show
that Marx realised that he must start from some basic
assumption, and this was his basic assumption or
'principle'. But 'work' does not *always* create wealth
and the consequences of his theory when applied have
been disastrous, the latest examples being Cuba and
Chile. Nevertheless Marxist theory was and is acclaimed
as 'scientific'.

However, Marx's basic assumption is one with which
many people agree, that work produces results assumed

[1] *Capital*, ed. F. Engels, Swan Sonnenschein, 1908.

to be necessarily good. For instance, it is said of the Germans that they work harder than the British and therefore their economy is in a sounder state. Yet in the 1970s the amount of physical effort being expended by Russians, Chinese or Indians may be much greater than that expended by the Germans, the Swiss or the Americans. It is plainly not a question of how much work is done, but of how effective that particular work is in achieving its given ends, which we would take as being to satisfy the customer who will pay no more than the product is worth to him. All who agree with Adam Smith's central dictum that 'Consumption is the sole end and purpose of all production' must accept that it is demand not cost which determines relative values.

. . . and Adam Smith was right
When we turn our attention to the consumer, it would seem obvious that the more an individual can satisfy his choices, the richer he will be. In the 20th century more people on the face of this earth have more choices and a larger ability to satisfy them than in any previous age. Why is this so? Adam Smith, again, tells us:

> 'This division of labour, from which so many advantages are derived, is not originally the effect of any human wisdom, which foresees and intends that general opulence to which it gives occasion. It is the necessary, though very slow and gradual, consequence of a certain propensity in human nature which has in view no such extensive utility: the propensity to truck, barter and exchange one thing for another . . .
>
> *Whether this propensity be one of those original principles* in human nature, of which no further account can

be given; or whether, as seems more probable, it be the necessary consequence of the faculties of reason and speech, it belongs not to our present subject to enquire . . .'[1] (My emphasis.)

It is my purpose here to study the possibility that voluntary exchange is a fundamental principle. Adam Smith also wrote:

'The uniform, constant and uninterrupted effort of every man to better his condition, the principle from which public and national, as well as private opulence is originally derived, is frequently powerful enough to maintain the natural progress of things towards improvement, in spite of both the extravagance of government and of the greatest errors of administration . . .'[2]

If we are to better our condition, we must be free to make the best use of our own efforts, to produce what *others* will want and to spend the proceeds on the products of others that satisfy us most. Every voluntary transaction is intended to be to the mutual benefit of both buyer and seller since one or other would soon withdraw if he found the exchange did not 'better his condition'.

When asked by a disciple if there were one single word which could serve as a principle of conduct for life, Confucius[3] replied 'Perhaps the word "reciprocity" will do'. May we interpret Confucius as agreeing that voluntary exchange is a principle?

When governments keep markets free, it becomes

---

[1] *The Wealth of Nations*, Vol. i.
[2] *The Wealth of Nations*, Vol. i.
[3] Lin Yutang, *The Wisdom of Confucius*, Michael Joseph, 1958.

necessary for each producer to discover what services or products are most required and to produce them at least cost. Others will have to do likewise for their own requirements, thereby producing a division of labour which widens choice. Where all stand to gain from this widening of choice, we see the wealth-creating possibilities of reciprocity or voluntary exchange.[1] The more effective the division of labour, the stronger the demand for 'protection' or 'subsidy' by defenders of threatened interests whether manufacturers, farmers or trade unions. The moment governments yield to such special pleading they embark on a descending spiral of diminishing choice for the generality of consumers.

Human beings often take a short view. They tend to see themselves as producers—workers, managers, investors—and fail to see that their interests as consumers are far more important to their economic welfare. The demand for government intervention invariably amounts to a call for politicians to protect everyone as a producer, against everybody as a consumer. Not only is this futile, it is a highly dangerous exercise setting up forces that can wreck society. Once again good intentions without understanding lead to opposite results from those intended.

So long as everyone exchanges that which he desires less for that which he desires more, the community must benefit. Voluntary exchange must be beneficial to both parties. It is the basis of profit and wealth

[1] Some American writers have recently returned to the word 'catallaxy' as preferable to 'economy' in emphasising the pervasive nature of exchange: Ludwig von Mises, *Human Action*, William Hodge, 1949. 'Catallactics or the Science of Exchange' was first used by Whately in *Introductory Lectures on Political Economy*, London, 1831.

creation. This communal or general increase in wealth as the result of exchange presupposes a framework of law and order which people are more likely to accept with honesty and integrity where everyone has a creative outlet for his natural effort to 'better his condition'.

Those who argue for free markets are often thought to be callous and uncaring about the poorer sections of the community. The truth is that the competitive system advocated by Adam Smith in practice enriches the choices *especially* of the less well-off, as Ludwig von Mises has explained:

> 'The characteristic feature of capitalism that distinguished it from pre-capitalistic methods of production was its new principles of marketing. Capitalism is not simply mass production, but *mass production to satisfy the needs of the masses*. The arts and crafts of the good old days catered almost exclusively to the wants of the well-to-do. But the factories produce cheap goods for the many. Big business, the target of fanatical hatred on the part of all contemporary governments and self-styled intellectuals, acquired and preserved its business only because it works for the masses.'[1]

How much choice?

If it is true that the more voluntary exchanges the richer the community will become, the duty of government must be to maximise individual choice. This does not mean either the 'permissive' society or that everyone's choice can be unrestricted. Unlimited choice can

---

[1] 'On Liberty and Property', a lecture to the Mont Pelerin Society, 1958.

be available only to a dictator who can gratify every whim at the expense of the choice of his subjects.

Nor is our goal the same as anarchy. Government and legislation are essential. A good example of 'maximised choice' is the rule of the road which is a clearly accepted law enforcing a restriction applicable to *all* to keep to the left (or right). As a result the use of the road is maximised: so long as the rule applies to everyone equally, we avoid the 'law of the jungle' where a person with a powerful vehicle or tank might do as he liked at our expense.

Legislation designed to maximise choice is legislation designed to protect equally all members of a nation or society and their property. It is legislation designed to facilitate exchanges and is not easy to devise. The first step is for legislators to be aware that they must make laws based on principles.

I hope I have set out enough of my thinking over many years to justify offering the following as a possible principle: people will make the best use of the scarce resources in a community, and thereby increase wealth fastest, where voluntary exchange is at a maximum. If this is so, a chief role of government is to maximise individual choice which leads to voluntary exchange.

It is probably true that most governments genuinely attempt to achieve policies that will produce desirable results. The most general approach is that the best way to benefit the poorer sections of the community is at the expense of the richer who conveniently are in a minority as voters. But if the policies are wrong, if they are choice-reducing instead of choice-increasing, the consequences are made worse by further guessing, wrong assumptions and compromise. Having reduced choice, governments all too readily reduce it further

c

when the method employed inevitably does not produce the consequences hoped for. This step-by-step reduction in choice paves the way of Professor Hayek's 'road to serfdom'.[1]

If my basic principle of maximised choice for the individual is the key to growth and prosperity, the progressive reduction of choice at some stage leads inevitably to stagnation, confusion, disorder and some-times to chaos. I shall in later chapters apply this test to historical development and also to more recent events, both in Britain and elsewhere.

The competitive process

Before leaving theory, I wish to discover whether we need any other basic principles to guide economic policy. At least one is suggested by the requirement that to maximise choice government must ensure that markets are free, which means that competition prevails. Although competition can be painful for the less efficient or less competent, its vital importance is indicated by Professor Hayek who coined the phrase for competition as 'an optimum discovery procedure'. This dictum is so important that it might be regarded as a secondary principle. After all, it would be difficult to deny the following sequence:

   (i) we are all imperfect in knowledge and ability;

 (ii) we will therefore always be making mistakes;

(iii) there is no known perfect way of offering services or manufacturing products;

(iv) in meeting change, competition provides a method of trial and error which is most likely to reveal the best solution.

---

[1] *The Road to Serfdom*, Routledge, 1944.

All activity must, therefore, be subject to as much competition as possible. Remove the comparison of competition and the individual faced with a decision no longer has a benchmark or test of performance. With the constant development of technology and changes in demand, there is no substitute for the discovery procedure of competition. It follows that monopoly which unavoidably reduces alternatives, especially 'nationalisation' which is state-protected monopoly, must be harmful.

Where competition is rigorous, the consumer will be offered better services or lower prices or both. He therefore controls the situation. Only the successful will make profits and they will be the measure of the success of any individual in serving the community. Losses will represent relative failure. From personal experience, I can confirm that if an individual is not operating under competitive conditions it is impossible to establish efficiency, or even to find out if an activity is making a profit or a loss.

Business v. bureaucracy

Man's own development over recorded history is a study of the competitive process summed up as the survival of the fittest. Animal life has been developing for some 650 million years and as new forms of life have occurred, so the stronger have squeezed out the weaker. An example of a species which for some reason or other failed to meet competition is the dodo. The phrase 'as dead as the dodo' refers to the extinction of a bird which formerly flourished on the island of Mauritius in the Indian Ocean but which, having no predatory enemies, did not have to fly and over the centuries forgot how to do so. When man and the dog first came to the island, the dodo could not compete and soon succumbed.

Where there are no competitive forces human beings, also, tend to take things easily. This situation is typified by a bureaucracy. Without any competitive check, government departments spend vast sums of money on services which the public would not choose to pay for voluntarily. One result is that governments are tempted to spend beyond their means and cover part of the cost by creating money, which incidentally, as we shall see, causes inflation. This is part of the syndrome of economic failure which can be traced back to the reduction of individual choice by policies that over-rule voluntary exchange.

Business, which consists of an infinite variety of exchanges, cannot operate without honesty. The more complicated business becomes, the more necessary it is for honesty to prevail. Honesty is a form of certainty. It is apparent that the Quakers, who have a very strict code of honesty, played a major part in establishing the British joint stock banks. Was this a coincidence? These people trusted one another in a way that was possible for few others.

Successful endeavour, prosperity, 'the better life' stem not only from honesty and free markets but also from conscientious effort, that is, effort designed to serve others as customers for our labour or our product. Successful effort in a competitive market must 'care' about others. The same cannot be said of bureaucratic activity which by its nature mostly depends upon over-ruling individual choice in spending a large part of each individual's income.

I have argued that we cannot have a well-ordered, happy, compassionate and advancing society without understanding basic principles which relate economic cause to consequence. We now turn to some practical applications.

CHAPTER 2

Write it Down

THE NEED TO DOCUMENT THE CASE

It is one thing to discuss the theories behind alternative policies, but it is also necessary to explain how they can be put into effect without getting bogged-down in party politics. The general public's impression is that politics are at best a tiresome necessity. Politicians are generally assumed to be insincere, whilst compromise is probably accepted as a vocational hazard. Two hundred years ago, Adam Smith contrasted the ideal legislator 'whose deliberations ought to be governed by general principles which are always the same' with 'that insidious and crafty animal sometimes called a statesman or politician whose counsels are directed by the momentary fluctuations of affairs'.

If my contention is true that government policy-making is based on ignorance, or at best on guesswork, a change in government is unlikely to provide lasting relief to our trials. The analogy may be that of a craft being swept towards the rapids, and an election merely brings the prospect of somebody else's hand on the tiller. If economic salvation depended only on a change of party in power, we should surely be in economic heaven already. Mr Wilson's '100 days' in 1964–5 was supposed to bring perfection in place of '13 years of Tory misrule'. The practical result was that all our difficulties were made worse.

One more plan

Lord George-Brown, like countless politicians before him, thought he had only to make a 'plan' and all would be well. It is unlikely he was aware of previous similar attempts: few politicians realise there is almost nothing they can do which has not already been tried time and again. Despite Lord George-Brown's obvious sincerity and wish to do good, the effort exploded in his face because he did not understand what he was doing.

In May 1965, four months *before* the publication of *The National Plan*, the Institute of Economic Affairs published an Eaton Paper with the same title in which John Brunner unerringly pointed to its practical futility as a 'vague indication of aspirations'. In the event, the National Plan for 1964 to 1970 was published in September 1965, with heavy emphasis that it had been prepared 'in co-operation with private and nationalised industries'. Nine months later the Labour Government abandoned it in favour of an unplanned package of crisis measures, explaining that policy had been 'blown off course'. In his subsequent post-mortem, Brunner diagnosed the weakness as a 'yearning for certainty which must always prove chimerical'. If the future could be foreseen with certainty it could be planned with confidence. It is because the future is always full of surprises that we need the discovery procedure of competitive trial and error.

Political decisions based on guesswork or wrong assumptions are legion. 'Foreign aid', 'welfare', subsidised rents, 'fair wage' laws, all have worthy objectives, but so long as the underlying principles are not understood the objectives are not achieved. Worse still, when results turn out the opposite, blame is put on a failure to apply the legislation correctly or with sufficient vigour. In such cases, more of the same 'remedies' results only in surer deterioration in the economy. That is why we need to start from the root causes of economic failure.

The failure of politicians

Many politicians and commentators believe there can be little variation between the policies of Government and Opposition. Since things are the way they are, and since vast sums of money are required to continue policies which are already decided and which cannot easily be changed, the policies pursued by the two parties cannot be very different. Two classic examples are Labour's continuance of Conservative mistakes in atomic energy after 1964 and the Conservative persistence with Labour's Concorde after 1970.

People will tend to vote for the opposition party once the other has been in power long enough to demonstrate that it cannot correct the situation, or produce the desired result. In this sense party voting is negative. One may legitimately ask 'Is anyone in charge?' or 'must the boat go over the rapids?' There may be slight variations in the alternative policies put forward to avoid disaster, but the choice the voter has is very slim.

One self-imposed trouble of politicians is that they are very busy and have little, if any, time for research. MPs have an impossible job when government becomes involved in every detail of our lives. Laws reach the statute book without proper discussion. This result is inevitable so long as parliament is trying to do work which no parliament can ever do.

The average politician does little or no research, but

without a sound understanding of principles he is unlikely to be constructive. It is easy to be negative and easiest of all for a politician in opposition to be critical when the ruling party has been in government long enough to have proved itself no better than the last. This is why politicians spend much time attacking each other and the public gets bored with the process. Mr Enoch Powell is one of the exceptions to the rule that politicians seldom do research. He does make reasoned speeches based on research which in consequence achieve wide publicity and have won him many followers.

'Research' publications issued by a political party are bound to be biased, and therefore attract little attention from the press and the intellectual world. The many political compromises in producing a 'package deal' will probably mean that the policy cannot resist increasing taxation and government action, thereby helping to build up the syndrome which is so harmful. Because government decision-making is not based on principles, an inevitable result is that countless 'deals' are made to meet the demands of pressure groups. As each group seeks to achieve privileges at the expense of others, and as all the others are doing exactly the same, the ultimate result must be a highly uneconomic system based on restraint and compulsion. Lacking fundamental principles as guides, the politician and his party organisation are like amateur explorers marching in step to an unknown destination without a map, navigational equipment or any real knowledge of the stars.

The impact of ideas
Almost as though he were predicting the influence of

his own ideas since the war, Lord Keynes wrote:

> '. . . the ideas of economists and political phil-
> osophers, both when they are right and when they
> are wrong, are more powerful than is commonly
> understood. Indeed the world is ruled by little
> else. Practical men, who believe themselves to be
> quite exempt from any intellectual influences, are
> usually the slaves of some defunct economist . . .
> soon or late, it is ideas, not vested interests, which
> are dangerous for good or evil.'[1]

Those whom Keynes saw as wielding influence are the
intellectuals who pick up new ideas (or forgotten old
ideas) and put them across in the news and opinions
they propagate in the press, radio, television and books.
These are the journalists, script-writers, academics,
authors and other 'experts'.

The politician is apt to be an avid reader of the press.
He wishes to gauge 'public opinion' as a way of winning
or holding on to power, prestige and votes. Yet so long
as he hopes to become a leader by being a follower, he
must eventually fail. To be a leader requires an understanding of fundamental ideas and how to put them
into practice, probably running counter to current
fashions, as the wide following of Mr Powell may
perhaps prove to some even who do not always agree
with him.

The quotation from Keynes implies that backroom
research can be effective 'for good or evil', and the
undoubted influence of Adam Smith and Karl Marx
provide contrasting examples of this process. The
success of new ideas depends on at least one person not

---

[1] *The General Theory of Employment, Interest and Money*, Macmillan,
1936.

only understanding the case, but also writing it down for others to study. If the report is convincing and preferably has a good summary, and perhaps even a summary of a summary, it will be read, reviewed and increasingly taught to others. In due time, it will begin to produce consequences.

Perhaps the most obvious of all political mistakes is the belief that it is possible to make the poor richer by taking from the rich.

> 'The redistribution of incomes has this remarkable feature, that the majority of both its champions and its opponents believe that it happens in a sense that it does not . . . The reason is that though our system does indeed tax the rich exceptionally heavily, the magnitude of the total effect is misconceived. There simply are not enough rich to make much difference . . . The modern high-taxing, high-spending state does not obtain its vast revenues from the rich but from heavy taxes on all citizens, including the poor.'[1]

The evidence reviewed later indicates that such policies will cause confusion and may benefit the poor only briefly, if at all. It is, on the other hand, possible to establish an economy in which the choices of the poor are maximised, and it is the principles which produce this consequence that are not understood. Having decided our objectives, we must work out the principles which will produce the desired outcome and then write the result down clearly, as I try to do in Chapter 6.

[1] Arthur Shenfield, 'Trial by Taxation', in *Right Turn*, Churchill Press, 1970.

What is 'politically impossible'?

If Socrates was right in saying that no one does wrong
on purpose, then differences about what is right are
more probably due to lack of understanding than to
villainy. Thus it is confusion over such words as 'aid',
'welfare', 'subsidy' that has led both political parties in
Britain astray. Any discussion about radically alternative policies invariably produces the reply that it is
'politically impossible'.

For example, from the inception of the British Egg
Marketing Board in 1957 until its demise in 1968, I
was one of very few who tried to point out that the
'subsidy' was leading to harmful consequences for the
very producers it was intended to help. I was constantly
told that I must compromise and conform, and that
since it was 'politically impossible' to get rid of the
Board and the subsidy, we had to learn to live with
them. I persevered in making speeches and circulating
memoranda until by 1967 the consequences of the
Board and the subsidy were so painful that it suddenly
became 'politically possible' to get rid of both. Thus
the case had been documented and was ready to
influence events as soon as circumstances made people
think again.

Among policies which were once thought 'politically
impossible' we may recall the introduction of commercial television (1955), the abolition of resale price
maintenance (1964), legislation on trade unions (1971),
floating exchange rates (1972), freeing the price of
gold (1972), phasing out rent subsidies (1973). All
were documented long before the changes came about.
Policies still thought 'politically impossible' which will
equally certainly be introduced as the case is more
fully documented and better understood include the

replacement of public monopoly welfare services (especially medical care and education) by private competing suppliers, loans in place of grants for university students (and other categories), denational-isation of state industries, and the drastic reduction of government spending and taxation.

I try to set out the case for these and other radical reforms in Chapter 6. Meanwhile I suggest that what seems in 1973 truly politically impossible is the con-tinuation of post-war 'consensus' policies that have culminated in a 'Conservative' government breaking all records for reducing choice by increasing public expenditure and imposing controls over prices, wages, salaries, profits, while inflation continues at a higher level than ever before.

An explosive example

It may be difficult to win attention for a most convinc-ing case for radical reform unless it is written down. When in 1940, Dr (now Sir) Barnes Wallis wanted government support for his large bomb to destroy the Mohne Dam, which supplied power and water for the Ruhr industries,[1] he went to see Lord Beaverbrook and explained the technique he proposed. 'You know how short we are of staff', said Beaverbrook, 'this thing's *only a theory*. We'd have to stop work on other projects to make it, and then it might be a flop.'

Here was a classic example of the businessman's natural scepticism of academics and theories. Wallis had a keen ally in Sir Arthur (later Lord) Tedder, chief of research and development at the Air Ministry; but after he left for the Middle East Wallis was told that the Air Council seemed wary of big bombs.

[1] *Reader's Digest*, May 1968, p. 176 (my emphasis).

Indeed, the verdict was that anyone who thought of ten-ton bombs was 'mad'. Wallis decided to write a treatise on his bomb, explaining each step so lucidly that a layman could follow it. The resulting book was then sent to 70 influential men in science, politics and the RAF.

The first result was a visit from a secret serviceman who reprimanded Wallis for sending through the post what had apparently become 'vital and very secret'. Shortly afterwards, Sir Henry Tizard, scientific adviser to the Ministry of Aircraft Production, felt moved to form a committee to study the proposal. The consequences we all know.

Even if it were true that those in authority will not listen and do not want to learn, each worsening spasm in the economy will make more people willing to listen. As taxes rise and controls encroach deeper on individual choice, more ears will be attentive.

Doubters will say, 'even if you are correct in arguing that we must think out the right policy, there is not time; things are so desperate that we must take action now'. Since this is tantamount to saying that politicians must act without thinking first, we must turn to history to show how thinking can help.

CHAPTER 3

Look Back at History
LEARNING FROM MANY LANDS IN MANY AGES

The only lesson we learn from history, said G. K. Chesterton, is that we learn nothing from history. Not only does this seem to be true but, if human development were governed by chance, there surely would be no lessons to be learnt. If history is the haphazard outcome of accident, there would seem little we can do to alter the course of events in our own time.

The beginnings of understanding
My study of many episodes in the past has convinced me that man's decision-making can and does govern events. My reading of history suggests that there are principles which can be learned and which can help us achieve certain consequences. And if governments fly in the face of these principles, we can predict the kind of troubles that will follow.

I propose to review some of the extensive historical evidence in the light of my primary principle that when choice is maximised increased prosperity follows. If my basic thinking is correct, we will find that where governments have deliberately reduced individual choice—often with the best possible intentions—the increase in prosperity will be slowed down or even reversed. Sometimes when governments have vigorously pursued a policy of reducing choice, prosperity has vanished into chaos—and on at least one occasion into oblivion.

SOME PAINFUL LESSONS

After 1918, when the American Government was unwinding its war-time controls, Mary G. Lacy (librarian of the Department of Agriculture in Washington) was invited to review the history of official efforts to fix prices. The result was a paper entitled 'Food Control During Forty-Six Centuries, A Contribution to the History of Price Fixing'. She concluded:

> 'The history of government limitation of price seems to teach one clear lesson: that in attempting to ease the burdens of the people in a time of high prices by artificially setting a limit on them, the people are not relieved but only exchange one set of ills for another which is greater. Among these ills are the withholding of goods from the market . . . the dividing of the community into two hostile camps, one only of which considers that the government acts in its interests, and the practical difficulties of enforcing such limitation in prices . . .'

Mary Lacy showed that in trying to deal with inflation governments had on many occasions deliberately interfered with individual choice. She summarised numerous examples of government interference which, despite the best intentions for 'the good of the people', produced the opposite results of impoverishing them and reducing choice. The Greeks, some 2,500 years ago, coined the word 'stasis' to describe such traumatic occasions.

The Roman Empire

The classic example of the attempt by government to improve the lot of the people by restricting their choice is that of the Emperor Diocletian about the year AD 300. He was faced with the familiar problem of rising prices in the wake of an increase in the quantity of money and a debasement in its value. As the historian Duray tells us:

> 'Under the impression that to give to a piece of metal whatever value they liked, it sufficed to engrave the Emperor's name upon it, the Roman Government had ended by putting in circulation pieces of "silver" and "gold" which contained neither silver nor gold . . . Very high prices resulted therefore from the depreciation of the currency.'[1]

The modern reader will not, therefore, be surprised to know that in the preface to his famous Edict of AD 301, Diocletian declared:

> 'All men know that articles of traffic and objects of daily use have attained exorbitant prices, four or eight times their true value, or even more than that; so that, through the avarice of monopolies, the provisioning of our armies becomes impossible.'

Miss Lacy quotes the historian Abbott as follows:

> 'In his effort to bring prices down to what he considered a normal level, Diocletian did not content himself with such half measures as we are trying in our attempts to suppress combinations in restraint of trade, but he boldly fixed the maximum prices at which beef, grain, eggs, clothing, and other articles should be sold, and prescribed the penalty of death for anyone who disposed of his wares at a higher figure.'[2]

[1] *History of Rome*, Vol. 6, Kegan Paul, 1883.
[2] *The Common People of Ancient Rome*, Scribner, New York, 1911.

D

By today's standards, Diocletian's task was relatively simple. We are told that he had to fix prices for no more than between 700 and 800 items, which were all that were commonly traded in those days, along with the wages of teachers, advocates, bricklayers, tailors, weavers, physicians and humbler callings.

The modern reader will hardly be surprised to hear that the result of such coercive efforts to dictate artificial prices for goods and services was total failure. In the more dramatic words of Lactantius, a contemporary historian writing within a decade or so of the event, the considered verdict on Diocletian was as follows:

> 'After many oppressions which he put in practice had brought a general dearth upon the empire, he set himself to regulate the prices of all vendible things. There was also much blood shed upon very slight and trifling accounts; and the people brought provisions no more to markets, since they could not get a reasonable price for them; and this increased the dearth so much, that at last after many had died by it, the law itself was laid aside.'[1]

One brighter note to emerge from Miss Lacy's catalogue of repeated error was that Diocletian had better success in his subsequent effort with the alternative policy of currency reform, which might be regarded as the ancient equivalent of monetary policy—to which I believe present-day governments will yet have to return before inflation is tackled at its monetary source. Even so, it was left to Emperor Constantine to restore confidence and stability by

[1] *A Relation of the Death of the Primitive Persecutors*, Amsterdam, 1687.

re-introducing a reliable currency based on gold which the people knew could not be debased for the convenience of politicians—as could paper or other substitute currencies.

On such efforts to restrict choice by controlling prices, in a vain effort to combat the fall in value of a debased currency, another Roman historian, M. Rostovtzeff, wrote:

> 'The same expedient had often been tried before him and was often tried after him. As a temporary measure in a critical time, it might be of some use. As a general measure intended to last, it was certain to do great harm and to cause terrible bloodshed, without bringing any relief. Diocletian shared the pernicious belief of the ancient world in the omnipotence of the state, a belief which many modern theorists continue to share with him and with it.'[1]

Usury in England

If 'choice maximised' means the most rapid increase in prosperity, any restriction of it should be viewed with suspicion. Yet in the eighth century Christians were forbidden to lend or borrow money by charging or paying interest. Since this ecclesiastical law did not prevent people wishing to borrow, it is not surprising that the Jews, who had no foolish inhibitions about payment, became bankers and money lenders.

In 1364 Edward III empowered the City of London to issue an ordinance against usury and an Act of Parliament with a similar objective was passed in 1390. As one might suppose, those who wished to lend or

[1] *The Social and Economic History of the Roman Empire*, OUP, Second Edition, 1957.

borrow found many loopholes in the law which resulted in the more stringent Act of 1487, which proved equally vain and was repealed in 1495. Although it condemned usury, it allowed the '*poena conventionalis*', or '*usura punitora*', thereby sanctioning what it was specially designed to forbid. Henry VIII legalised the lending of money at interest up to 10 per cent in 1545. In 1552 another attempt was made to prohibit usury, but when it failed Queen Elizabeth legalised the lending of money at interest with the limit still at 10 per cent. In 1624 this limit was reduced to 8 per cent and in 1651 to 6 per cent. From then on the argument over the legality of charging interest concentrated merely on the rate, until the restrictions were removed altogether in 1854. What is certain is that if an artificially low rate of interest had been successfully enforced in the 19th century, capital investment would have been held back and the growth in standards of living retarded.

Wat Tyler

Every schoolboy knows, or used to know, about Wat Tyler and his rebellion of 1381, but probably few appreciate that it arose from an attempt by the British Government to freeze wages.

Sir Arthur Bryant[1] tells how Black Death or bubonic plague reduced the population by about half in 25 years. The resulting labour shortage naturally led to a spectacular rise in wages, which parliaments, controlled by landowers, tried to prevent by punitive ordinances and legislation. In these days of increasing strike action, it is interesting to read:

[1] *The Fire and the Rose*, Collins, 1965.

'In the thirty years after the first post-Black Death statute against what Council and parliament called "the malice of labourers", nearly nine thousand cases of wage enforcement were tried by the courts and in nearly all judgment was given in the employer's favour.'

Not surprisingly, Sir Arthur tells us: 'These Statutes of Labourers aroused bitter class-feeling.' Despite repressive legislation we read of evasion by

'. . . surly villeins standing idle in the fields or trampling in angry companies to the nearest town to sell their labour to those who would pay highest for it.'

The Pilgrims in New England
The coming of the pilgrims to the New England coast in 1620 marked the first 'socialist' experiment in America. It failed within three years when the settlers discovered that, for their very survival, they had to turn to what we now know as the free market system because minimised choice did not work. We can still learn a valuable lesson from this early failure of 'socialism', which I believe is best described as a system of minimised individual choice.

Before landing, the Pilgrims entered into what is known as the Mayflower Compact, under which Plymouth was set up as a share-the-wealth community. Nobody owned anything and whatever was produced became common property. They lived under this system from the desperate first winter of 1620–21 until the hungry Spring of 1623, when they changed to a market system. The reason was explained by William Bradford (one of the leading original Pilgrims and second governor of Plymouth Colony) in a tract entitled *Of Plimoth Plantation*. He describes how common ownership

> '. . . was found to breed much confusion and discontent and ritard imployment that would have been to their benefits and comforte. For the young men that were most able and fitte for labor and service did repine that they should spend their time and strength to worke for other mens wives and children, without any recompense. The strong . . . had no more in devision of victails and cloaths than he that was weake . . . Upon the poynte all being to have alike, and all to doe alike, they thought themselves in the like condition, and one as good as another. And so, if it did not cut off those relations that God hath set amongst men, yet it did at least much diminish and take of the mutuall respects that should be preserved amongst them.'

Instead of a Thanksgiving feast in the fall of 1622, there was starvation and a collapse of morale.

> 'So they begane to thinke how they might raise as much corne as they could . . . that they might not still thus languish in misere. At last, after much debate of things, the governor gave way that they should set corne every man for his own particular . . . And so assigned to every family a parcell of land . . . This had very good success for it made all hands very industrious, so as much more corne was planted than other waise would have bene.'

The Thanksgiving feast in the fall of 1623 was, in plain truth, a celebration of their deliverance from socialism. Bradford philosophised:

'The experience that was had in this commone course and condition, tried sundrie years, and that amongst Godly and sober men, may well evince the Vanitie of that conceite of Plato's and other ancients, applauded by some of later times, that the taking away of propertie and bringing in communitie into a commone wealth would make them happy and flourishing; as if they were wiser than God!'

It was this freeing of individual choice for consumers no less than producers that prepared the way for the miracle of American economic development.

I would certainly claim the constitution of 1787 as a further step which helped to maximise choice in the USA. Its provisions were thought out with great care and reflected the accumulated wisdom of the time. It was the child of much tribulation and conflict, as had been Urukagina's new laws (below, p. 48) and our own Magna Carta. The constitution was based on the sanctity of the individual and the protection of private property. Once again, it was an attempt to maximise choice by preventing any individual exercising his freedom at the expense of others. Again, we find that the nation that has applied these principles in government prospers. Is this chance, or is there a definite cause-and-effect relationship?

For 150 years after the constitution, the US economy prospered. Maximised choice resulted in more and more voluntary exchanges and stimulated an unprecedented increase in wealth. It is no coincidence that this miracle has faltered in recent years as American governments have exerted increasing powers of taxation and control over industry and trade.

Competitive mail services

The postal services have always been considered a natural government monopoly. What is surprising is the number of occasions individuals have challenged this monopoly and produced a better service.[1]

The originator of the first penny post was William Dockwra in 1680. He introduced the world's first stamp, a hand-struck triangular design bearing the words 'Penny Post Paid'. He provided insurance on anything up to £12 at no extra charge and established the first house-to-house delivery service with ten deliveries a day. He was so successful that the Duke of York, who operated the government Post Office service in London, sued him for infringing the state monopoly. It took two years to shut down Dockwra and he was fined £100 for contempt. The state took over his collecting stations and converted most of them into branches of the GPO.

In 1709 another adventurer, Charles Povey, set up a halfpenny carriage, with postmen who called to collect as well as deliver. Penny posts began to spring up everywhere and by 1800 over 2,000 of them had been established in the British Isles. A man named Williamson set up a Penny Post in Scotland and it was 17 years before the GPO took him over when, instead of being fined, he was awarded a pension.

In his book *Men Against the State*,[2] James J. Martin reports that in the USA:

'From 1841 to 1845, steady inroads on the revenues of the federal post office department were made

---

[1] This summary is based on a study published in *Innovator*, Box 3478, Los Angeles, Ca. 90034, USA.

[2] Ralph Myles Publishers, 1970.

by private enterprise companies. It was a source
of embarrassment to the Democratic Administration of the period to see mail companies making
profits from carrying letters for 5 and 10 cents each,
while providing a service somewhat more expedi-
tious than that furnished by the federal postal
system.'

Here was competition acting highly efficiently as 'a
discovery procedure'. The predictable government
response was a bill whose sponsor frankly explained

'that there was to be no attempt at competing
with these firms; they were to be put out of
business by "penal enactment".'

Time and again we see that people in government
prefer to use their power to prevent choice and
competition rather than to direct their efforts to
improving their services and leaving customers with
freedom to go elsewhere.

Encore in France
In a society where choice is maximised, each individual
exercises power by his decisions to buy or sell on terms
he chooses. Such freedom enables him to protect
himself against bad government or other oppressive
monopoly power. One such choice, which incompetent
governments periodically try to take away from their
citizens, is the ability to buy and sell gold. Many say
that gold has no 'value' except in the manufacture of
ornaments, plate and jewellery. But, as we shall see,
any product (or 'money') has a value that can be truly
assessed only by the readiness of others to offer their
goods and services in exchange.

In his introduction to a study of inflation in France,[1] the American writer Henry Hazlitt recalls that in 1789 the Minister of Finance, Necker, fought for financial rectitude in the hope of keeping France faithful to sound monetary principles. Mr Dickson White says of Necker:

> 'Anyone today reading his prophecies of the evils sure to follow such a [paper] currency would certainly ascribe to him a miraculous foresight, were it not so clear that his prophetic power was due simply to a knowledge of natural laws revealed by history.'

All the age-old arguments in favour of the creation of money were brought forward, but some still remembered an earlier experience of 1716 when John Law persuaded the French Regent that he could restore French industry from the depression caused by the extravagance and corruption of Louis XIV by starting a bank to issue notes. The Bank's notes soon went to a premium, Law having publicly declared at the outset that any banker deserved death who issued notes without sufficient security to answer all demands. Alas, both he and the Regent soon forgot this wise maxim and their initial success led them to think that a paper currency which could supplement gold and silver coin might entirely supersede it.

The Bank was so successful that it was granted a monopoly of tobacco and the sole right of refining gold and silver. It effectively became the Royal Bank of France and promptly issued new notes to the amount of 1,000,000,000 livres. This departure from sound

[1] Andrew Dickson White, *Fiat Money—Inflation in France*, Foundation for Economic Education, USA, 1959.

principles was quickly followed by the familiar symptoms of inflation. Bread, meat and vegetables rose to
record prices and the wages of labour climbed in
proportion. By 1720 the government felt driven by
popular outcry to suspend the convertibility of notes
into gold and then to forbid the holding of gold or
even the buying of jewellery, plate and precious
stones.

Yet despite these experiences, revolutionary France
in 1790 behaved as if it was deliberately staging an
encore: the government once again embarked irre-
trievably on an inflationary process by new issues of
paper money. At first a new issue was made of
400,000,000 livres based on the security of the con-
fiscated property of the church, which was supposed to
guarantee that the notes would 'soon be considered
better than the coin now hoarded and will bring it out
again into circulation'. Mirabeau even proposed to
repay the public debts by the issue of 2,400,000,000
livres in legal tender notes and to forbid the use of
specie in purchasing national lands. Once again the
predictable result followed: prices rose and gold began
to disappear from circulation. The blame was variously
put on brokers, the Bourbon family, speculators,
foreign merchants.

When in the early 1790s the appalling inflation
caused the government to run out of foreign money, it
resorted to a most fantastic auction of the contents of
the palace of Versailles, lasting three hundred and
fifty-one days. But selling assets can stave off bankruptcy
only for a short time. Meanwhile, Dickson White
reports:

'Enterprise received a mortal blow . . . This state

of things, too, while it bore heavily upon the monied classes was still more ruinous to those in moderate, and most of all to those in stricken, circumstances . . . These evils though great were small compared to those far more deep-seated signs of disease which now showed themselves throughout the country.'

Thrift gave way to gambling and extravagance among the rich, while the washer-women of Paris responded to the high soap price by demanding that the merchants who sold it should be punished by death. Marat thereupon suggested that the people might help themselves literally by hanging shopkeepers and plundering their stores.

In 1793 came the first real price and wage controls, Robespierre's so-called 'law of the maximum'. When it did not work, and goods disappeared from the markets, the guillotine was worked overtime in a vain attempt to enforce the law. Punishment for selling paper assignats against gold or silver at less than their face value was 20 years' imprisonment in chains. Investment in foreign countries carried the death penalty.

Nevertheless, no government decree could prevent the louis d'or from recording the decline in the value of assignats. The gold louis, originally equivalent to 25 francs, was worth about 1,000 paper francs in September 1793 and over 7,000 six months later.

Dickson White's conclusion confirmed the findings of Mary Lacy in 1922 and of Professor Milton Friedman more recently.

'To cure a disease temporary in its character, a corrosive poison was administered, which ate out the vitals of French prosperity . . . It ended in the complete financial, moral and political prostration of France.'

One Frenchman who learned the correct lesson was Napoleon. When he was hard pressed financially and it was proposed to resort to paper money, he wrote to his minister, 'While I live, I will never resort to irredeemable paper.' Dickson White comments:

'He never did, and France, under his determination, commanded all the gold she needed. When Waterloo came, with the invasion of the Allies, with war on her own soil, with a change of dynasty, and with heavy expenses for war and indemnities, France on a specie basis experienced no severe financial distress.'

A footnote to the inflation in revolutionary France, where price-fixing finally became a characteristic feature of the Reign of Terror, is that when Robespierre finally passed through the streets of Paris in the tumbrils of the executioners, the mob jeered 'There goes the dirty maximum'.

Hunger and history
Parmalee Prentice, a son-in-law of the first Rockefeller, in 1951 published a study[1] which described the dismal quality and quantity of foods available to the human race until the establishment of the Enclosure Acts in England at the end of the 18th century. These Acts may appear to have restricted choice by combining individual strips of land into larger holdings. In practice they had the opposite effect by protecting

[1] *Hunger and History*, Caxton Printers, 1951.

private property and enabling farmers to choose for themselves what land, crops and livestock to cultivate.

Communal farming had previously prevented a good farmer from segregating his cattle from the animals of the bad farmers, while under the open field system crops could be grown only in rotation governed by age-old custom and weeds spread from the neglectful farmer to his neighbour's plots. The Enclosure Acts, by protecting private property and encouraging competition, set in motion forces which rapidly increased farming productivity. It was the resulting agricultural revolution which prepared the way for Britain's industrial revolution and if only the Indian government would learn this lesson it would do more to prevent hunger than by begging any amount of foreign aid to subsidise industrial 'development'.

The great German inflation

An American economist, Hans F. Sennholz, has shown[1] that the disastrous inflation in Germany after the First World War was remarkably like the French experience of the 1790s.

> 'Immediately after the war, the German Government, under the leadership of the Socialist party, embarked upon heavy expenditures for health, education and welfare. This added to the already heavy load on the Treasury for demobilisation expenses, the demands by the Armistice . . . While government expenditures rose by leaps and bounds, the revenue suffered a gradual decline; in October 1923, only 0.8 per cent of government expenses were covered by tax revenues . . . The depreciation

[1] 'Hyperinflation in Germany', in *The Freeman*, October 1970.

of the currency brought about the destruction of taxable wealth in the form of mortgages and bonds . . .'

Once again the blame was put on the balance of payments, speculators, and ultimately Jews. Professor Sennholz concludes with a prophecy:

'The specious argument that denies the presence of any inflation in terms of purchasing power or gold value may be expected to emerge in later phases of inflation when monetary authorities will desperately seek any argument that promises to hold them blameless.'

It was a Conservative minister in Britain who recently joined the chorus blaming 'property speculators' for the record inflation since 1972.

The Great Crash
The same author has written[1] about the great slump of the early 1930s which he compares with the business cycles that have plagued the American economy since 1820.

'In each case, Government had generated a boom through easy money and credit, which was soon followed by the inevitable bust . . . The spectacular crash of 1929 followed five years of reckless credit expansion by the Federal Reserve System under the Coolidge Administration.'

To meet a decline in business in 1924, the Reserve Bank suddenly created some $500 million of new money which led inevitably to a bank credit expansion of over

[1] 'The Great Depression', in *The Freeman*, October 1969.

$4,000 million in less than one year. The immediate effect was a temporarily agreeable economic boom. Predictably, when the threat of inflation loomed up, the authorities provoked the worst world slump ever by equally suddenly reducing the supply of money and raising protective tariffs, which invited retaliation from other countries and all but throttled international trade. Even such a classic case of government folly, however, has not prevented the legend that the world slump was caused by the failure of the free market!

In an effort to teach the correct lesson from this bit of history, Professor Friedman[1] has renamed the Great Depression the 'great contraction', thereby underlining the responsibility of the monetary authorities for their boom-and-bust excesses.

Another crash

Another method used by governments to reduce choice is to 'nationalise' a particular activity and to inhibit competition from private companies. An interesting and little-known test of public enterprise was provided by the Labour Government in 1930. Two large airships were built, one by the state and one by a private firm. One was finished long before the other and crossed the Atlantic and back; while the other on its maiden flight crashed in flames, killing all but six on board. There are no prizes for guessing which of the two was built by the state!

James Leasor in his story of this drama[2] tells how again and again during the building of the state airship wrong business decisions and even wrong technical

---

[1] *The Counter-Revolution in Monetary Theory*, Occasional Paper 33, IEA, 1970.

[2] *The Millionth Chance*, Hamish Hamilton, 1957.

decisions were made and covered up for political reasons. Compared with the privately built R.100 which successfully flew to Canada and back and altogether covered more than 20,000 miles with only normal wear and tear, the state-built R.101 cost twice as much and crashed on its maiden flight to India after just managing to get across the Channel to France.

The detailed case-study shows up the error of describing such heavy-footed state operations as 'public enterprises' when they neither benefit the public nor display true enterprise. There is some evidence that the R.101 crashed because it was overloaded, especially with the Air Minister's luggage which appears to have increased the maximum payload by *50 per cent* because he was privileged to exceed the limit of 10 lb imposed on everyone else. In this case, we may cite the tragedy as an example of politicians defying economic law and the law of gravity at one and the same time!

The story of two railroads

Professor Howard Stephenson, formerly of Boston University, presented another case study[1] of 'public' and private enterprise in the form of a comparison between two Canadian railroads, the privately-run Canadian Pacific and the nationalised Canadian National. Both had many ancillary activities in road and water transport, but competition was not entirely fair as exemplified by advantages the state conceded to its railroad in air transport.

The comparison of financial results over 18 years, from 1941 to 1958, revealed that where one company earned a profit of $669 million the other suffered a loss of $663 million. Again, there is no prize for guessing

[1] 'A Tale of Two Railroads', *The Freeman*, September 1960.

E

which was the result of nationalisation. But it might surprise some readers to hear that in addition to paying its shareholders almost $370 million, the private enterprise company also paid a similar sum in taxation, in contrast to the nationalised company's charge of over $660 million against taxation. No wonder politicians find competition an uncomfortable 'discovery procedure'.

SOME SUCCESS STORIES

I now want to turn to examples where man has not only learnt the right lessons from history but has managed to reverse the syndrome of failure by maximising rather than minimising choice. In each case there has been economic confusion or worse until the government deliberately attempted to increase choice, whereupon there was a striking increase in prosperity.

Urukagina of Lagash

The Sumerian civilisation, which began to flourish perhaps 6,000 years ago, fortunately developed writing on clay tablets some of which have survived sufficiently well to be deciphered recently.

Professor S. N. Kramer has written two excellent books[1] on Sumer which include researches into social reform and taxation. One of the most instructive fragments is the story of Urukagina of Lagash who ruled from about 2,350 BC. Previously a pervasive, obnoxious bureaucracy consisting of the Ruler and his Palace coterie had perfected the most sinister acts of tyranny and oppression. In the record of Urukagina's sweeping reforms, Professor Kramer tells us that 'we

[1] *From the Tablets of Sumer*, Falcon's Wing Press, Indian Hall, Colorado, 1956; and *The Sumerians*, University of Chicago Press, 1963.

find the word "freedom" used for the first time in man's recorded history'. What went before was the familiar sequence of high taxation, confiscation of property, and every conceivable infringement of personal rights and individual choice. A contemporary chronicler recorded that

> 'The rich, the big men, and the supervisors were getting richer and richer, at the expense of the less fortunate citizens, while from one end of the land to the other there were the tax collectors.'

What Urukagina did to correct this sorry state was to switch from a situation where choice was minimised, both because the law no longer protected the individual and because taxes were very high, to a policy which maximised choice. He established a rule of law that protected the rights of individuals, however humble, and prevented the abuse of power, however elevated. One significant legal innovation was his insistence that the Sumerian courts must 'make manifest to all, by means of the written word, the guilt for which the accused was punished'.

Urukagina swept away the oppressive bureaucracy, established honest weights and measures, including no doubt a reformed currency. The last word must be left to a contemporary historian:

> 'From one end of the land to the other . . . there were no tax collectors.'

It seems to me that enough can be gleaned from this episode to illustrate the contrast between minimised choice, which I equate with tyranny and stagnation, and maximised choice, which is more generally described as freedom and associated with prosperity.

Bengal: 1770 v. 1866

For a brief example of a lesson learnt from history, I can do no better than draw on Hunter's *Annals of Rural Bengal* from Mary Lacy's report.[1]

In 1770 Lower Bengal's rice harvest failed utterly, and fully a third of the population died. The government's response was to prohibit what it was pleased to term the monopoly of grain, thereby preventing prices from rising at once to their natural rates. Left to itself, Hunter argued,

> 'private enterprise would have stored up the general supply at the harvest with a view to realising a larger profit at a later period in the scarcity.'

In a free market prices would of course have risen, with the effect of compelling the population to reduce their consumption from the beginning and economise supplies. In this way the pressure of scarcity would be spread over the period to the next harvest, instead of being concentrated in the final months. As Mary Lacy pointed out, by prohibiting all speculation in rice, the government 'acted about as sagely as the skipper of a wrecked vessel who should refuse to put his crew upon half rations.' The predictable result of the government's well-meaning intervention was to intensify the impact of famine instead of alleviating it.

A century later the government of Bengal faced the famine of 1866 with a very different policy. Far from trying to check speculation, the government facilitated it by publishing weekly returns of prices in every district. As a result, the twin forces of choice and competition worked to bring about the transport of rice

[1] *Food Control During Forty-Six Centuries*, op. cit.

from areas of relative abundance to places of worst scarcity. Mary Lacy summarises the contrasting results which tell their own tale:

> 'In 1770 the price of grain, in place of promptly rising to three half-pence a pound as in 1865–66, continued at three farthings during the earlier months of the famine. During the latter months it advanced to two pence, and in certain localities reached fourpence.'

Thus, by refraining from curbs on consumer choice the government averted a repetition of the earlier national disaster.

Free trade—1846

Although understanding is essential before correct policies can be introduced, reform is often helped along by the influence of particular individuals and of favourable circumstances. The German economic miracle was one example of this combination and the repeal of the Corn Laws almost exactly 100 years earlier provided another.

The Corn Laws in 1815 prohibited (and in 1828 regulated) the import of wheat and other cereals into Britain unless the home price was high. The aim was to 'protect' both the landed interest and national defence after the Napoleonic Wars had shown the danger of depending on food imports in time of war. On the other hand, there were already thinkers and politicians who followed the teachings of Adam Smith in believing that free trade would be best to promote economic efficiency and, therefore, national strength in peace and war.

From 1820 the Manchester Chamber of Commerce

called again and again for free trade which would reduce the price of food and so enable the textile industry and other leaders of the industrial revolution to export more cheaply and advance the general prosperity of the country. Yet in spite of the efforts of Cobden, Bright and the Cheap Food League, when C. P. Villiers, the MP for Wolverhampton, moved a motion in the House of Commons every year to repeal the Corn Laws it was regularly rejected by very large majorities, even in the early 1840s.

Although the idea was increasingly widely understood, it was not until the failure of the potato crop in 1845 that British ports were thrown open to alternative supplies of food. Thereupon Robert Peel, as Conservative Prime Minister and defender of the agricultural interest, did what up to the last minute in 1846 was thought 'politically impossible'. He repealed the Corn Laws and thereby made possible half a century of prosperity based upon free trade which did more than anything else to reduce poverty by enlarging the choices open to the poor both in earning and in spending their rising incomes.[1]

The great increase in England's wealth cannot be ascribed to coal which had been there for millenia, nor to particular inventions which in many cases had first been made centuries earlier. My case is that the rapid exploitation of natural resources and human ingenuity was galvanised by the profit mechanism which, in turn, arose from the discovery procedure of competition and free markets. It was only as individuals were free to supply the demands (or 'choices') of other individuals, on a voluntary basis, that increments of wealth added up to a massive growth in wealth and standards of living.

[1] *The Long Debate on Poverty*, Readings 9, IEA, 1973.

A Swedish lesson

The history of Sweden between 1860 and 1913 offers another example of apparent prosperity, closely following a recognisable policy for the maximisation of individual choice. This example particularly illustrates how changes in legislation can come about because of the effort of an individual thinker working in a back room.

Dr F. A. Harper[1] has analysed this period and wrote:

> 'If we measure economic progress by the rise in output per hour of work, the golden age of Sweden was a period from the early 1860s to the outbreak of World War I . . . For that period as a whole, Sweden's average rate of increase was 2.76 per cent yearly, compounded. This far exceeds any level of increase in the United States for a sustained period of time.
>
> Economic progress in Sweden since 1913, though quite irregular, has been at a rate about one-third less than for the prior half century . . . wages left for the Swedish earner to spend on objects of his own choice were cut sharply by increasing taxes over the last half century.'

Sweden, like most other European nations before about 1860, was strongly 'mercantilist' and tried all sorts of controls in a vain effort to achieve higher living standards. The definite economic change both internally and externally in the early 1860s was, according to Harper, the result of the influence of the works of J. B. Say and later to the powerful influence of Frederic Bastiat, the noted French liberal.

[1] Institute for Humane Studies (unpublished paper).

Harper records that Bastiat's influence came to Sweden in the following way.

> 'A Swedish gentleman by the name of John August Gripenstedt, on one of his visits to France, made the acquaintance of Bastiat and established a friendship founded on deep admiration. Gripenstedt became a top political leader in Sweden using lines of reasoning quite clearly identified with Bastiat in his political speeches.'

By 1860, Harper tells us, Gripenstedt managed to:

> '. . . do away with all prohibitions against imports or exports, to abolish all export duties, to reduce the import tariffs for manufactured goods and to establish free trade in agricultural products . . . Sweden's golden age of half a century followed.'

The German economic miracle

We now come to the most fascinating example of all. In 1948 Germany was in a state of economic collapse. Inflation paralysed industry and business. Post-war reconstruction was at a standstill and morale could hardly have been lower. Suddenly, Dr Ludwig Erhard, the German Chancellor, introduced a new policy based on choice and competition with a result that has been called the 'Economic Miracle'.

At the end of the Second World War, Germany had been reduced to the physical level of an under-developed country, as films taken at the time demonstrate. The population of the western portion, about half of the Germany of 1939, was 13 per cent larger by the addition of some 12 million refugees. Although by 1947 other European countries were recovering rapidly from the war, the situation in Germany remained abysmal.[1] By 1948, industrial production was still only half the 1936 level. Exports were one-tenth and imports one-quarter the level in 1938. Infant mortality was high and food consumption low. The devastation was such that only those who had seen it could believe it.[2] I remember lunching with a German family near Cologne in 1947: the meal consisted of some cooked vegetables and the luxury, kept to the end, was a small piece of white bread.

Before the 1948 currency reform, the German economy was blanketed by a network of controls, especially price and wage controls intended to offset the effects of the substantial monetary expansion of the war. At artificially low prices, however, goods failed to move except via black markets. In Erhard's words, the economy 'had returned to a state of primitive barter'.[3]

Economic observers expected that Germany would be permanently weakened economically. Indeed, in the immediate post-war years policy-makers made it a definite objective of policy to reduce the country to a permanently rural state. The Morgenthau Plan envisaged that 10 million workers would be shifted from industry into agriculture,[4] while the Potsdam Declaration advocated the restriction of German industrial output to a level of some 45 per cent below that of 1936. The later Anglo-American Industrial

[1] United Nations Economic Commission for Europe, *Economic Survey of Europe in 1947*, Geneva, 1948.

[2] W. H. Chamberlain, *The German Phoenix*, Hale, London, 1963, Ch. 2.

[3] *Prosperity Through Competition*, Thames & Hudson, 1958, p. 12.

[4] H. Morgenthau, *Germany is our Problem*, Harper, New York, 1945.

Plan of 1946 would have permitted the level of output to equal that of 1936, although the population was larger.

It was against this bleak background that Dr Erhard introduced his radical economic reforms of July, 1948. They replaced the inflated Reichmarks with a smaller supply of Deutschemarks and threw 'into the waste-paper basket, at one swoop, hundreds of decrees, promulgating controls . . .'[1] The immediate impact of this release of market forces was striking.

> 'The black market suddenly disappeared. Shop windows were full of goods, factory chimneys were smoking, and the streets swarmed with lorries. Everywhere the noise of new buildings going up replaced the deathly silence of the ruins. If the state of recovery was a surprise, its swiftness was even more so.
>
> In all sectors of economic life, it began as the clock struck on the day of currency reform. Shops filled up with goods from one day to the next; the factories began to work. On the eve of currency reform the Germans were aimlessly wandering about their towns in search of a few additional items of food. A day later they thought of nothing but producing them. One day apathy was mirrored on their faces, while on the next the whole nation looked hopefully into the future.'[2]

There was, however, much opposition to the new policy. For the British Labour ministers, busy applying their favourite policies of controls, one can only imagine their consternation at Erhard's action. In

[1] Erhard, *op. cit.*, pp. 10, 11, 13.
[2] *Ibid.*, p. 13.

Germany, the trade unions called for a general strike and the civil service began secretly drafting new decrees for the re-establishment of controls.

The attitude of socialist economists was revealingly illustrated by the severe attack from Dr Thomas (now Lord) Balogh.[1] Within two years of the great experiment in freedom, he denounced the currency reform and its supporting programme for monetary stability as 'savage deflation'. This policy, he said,

> '. . . beggared the middle classes and the workers, just as they had been robbed by the great inflation of the First War. The instability of the German social system has irredeemably been intensified. The eventual political consequences cannot be estimated.'

The superiority of the pre-Erhard régime of direct controls was emphasised.

> 'Control over production and consumption represents the most effective and flexible means of imposing relative pressures, equivalent to localised deflation, on industry without incurring the need for a general cut in income, causing unnecessary hardship and unemployment . . . By direct controls, demand can be cut to fit in with productive or export/import bottlenecks and the resulting excess demand directed to innocuous uses . . .'

Finally, Balogh predicted the failure of the whole scheme.

[1] *Germany, an Experiment in Planning by the Free Price Mechanism,* Blackwell, Oxford, 1950.

'The German Government tried to apply to real-life an abstract, obsolescent and internally inconsistent economic theory . . . There are two tests of an economic policy—first, does it increase national income? Second, does it distribute the product justly? The German experiment failed in both.'

This partisan analysis provides a classic example of a mistaken assessment based on a preference for policies that reduce other people's choice. It is similar to the line of argument used by economists who advocate incomes policy which reduces choice without achieving the aim of solving inflation.

However, by 1956, Balogh was commending the German example to Britain's Conservative Government:

'Between 1950 and 1955 [West Germany] invested more than twice as much as Britain[1] . . . Real wages in England rose only 12.3 per cent since 1950 against 24 per cent in the US and 39 per cent in Germany.'[2]

But then even an unsympathetic intellectual would have to acknowledge that it was not quite a 'failure' for Germany to more than treble exports and almost double money incomes between 1949 and 1956 while the cost of living rose only 14 per cent.[3] By 1960, Balogh acknowledged that Germany had established itself as 'the unchallenged economic leader in Europe'[4] and went further to admit:

[1] *New Statesman*, 1 December, 1956.
[2] *New Statesman*, 19 November, 1957.
[3] Erhard, *op. cit.*, pp. 52, 69, 184, 228, 246.
[4] *The Free Trade Proposals*, edited by G. D. N. Worswick, Blackwell, 1960.

'The fact stands out that in Germany, France and Japan the improvement in workers' earnings and social benefits was at a rate two or three times as high, despite a worsening of the distribution of income, than in Britain.'

It was the classical liberal economist, Wilhelm Röpke, who drew the true lesson of Erhard's success.[1]

'Now there is much talk about the German miracle. For the economist there is no miracle. It is a very simple story of ending economic paralysis and disorder brought about by planning and inflation and ending it by sound economic order based on two things. First, the freedom of goods and markets, and second on discipline in the field of money . . . the idea was simple. The difficult thing was to put it into practice . . . the miracle was that this return to wisdom and common-sense was possible on the political and social levels and at a time in which collectivism and inflationism seemed to be triumphant. This had been the essence of National and Socialist economic policy during the Third Reich.'

As one of the intellectual inspirers, along with Professor Walter Eucken, of Erhard's policy, Röpke might be forgiven a parting quip and prophecy.

'It might be almost amusing today to collect all the wrong prophecies and desperate theories which have been invented in order to disprove the striking evidence of the German experiment . . . the Socialists, if they do not want to be defeated in

[1] 'Will West Germany's Free Enterprise System Survive?', *Commercial & Financial Chronicle*, New York, 14 June, 1962.

> the elections, have to assure that they believe in
> the market economy and a sound currency . . . so
> economic law has triumphed over Karl Marx.'

Although more recently German governments have
fallen victims to some of the wrong policies practised
elsewhere in Europe, for a time the success of Erhard's
reforms was proved by the anxiety of the German
Social Democrats to assure voters that they were no
longer a socialist party.

Understanding the key

From many centuries and diverse countries, I have
summarised case histories of circumstances where
tribulation has caused men to pause and think as a
necessary preliminary before acting to maximise choice.
The pages of history confirm that on the few occasions
when this has been done the results have been highly
beneficial.

It emerges that apparently isolated individuals in a
'backroom' can be tremendously effective for both
good and ill. Adam Smith, Karl Marx, Cobden,
Röpke, Eucken and Bastiat are all 'men of theory' who
have produced more far-reaching consequences than
they may dared to have hoped. The consequences have
been achieved not by weight of numbers, but often by
the understanding of individuals. In most cases this
understanding had been documented before it was
implemented.

One outstanding instance of the ability and power of
one man is the story of the farmer, Gideon, as told in
the Book of Judges. When the Midianites had beaten
the Israelites, Gideon, an Israelite of no great standing,
collected 32,000 men for battle to free his people. Being
a Jew he believed in a wise God, to whom he turned in

deep thought and prayer. The guidance he received
was as follows:

> 'The people that are with thee are too many for
> me to give the Midianites into their hands, lest
> Israel vaunt themselves against me, saying Mine
> own hand hath saved me.'

Instead, Gideon was told: 'Tell the people that all who
are afraid should return home' and 22,000 went home,
leaving 10,000. But God was still not satisfied and
required Gideon to select only 300.

Then by the simplest of strategies, with the surprise
use of trumpets and lights after dark and without
weapons, the Midianites were scared into flight.
Without a warlike stroke Gideon was shown how to win
the battle. Wisdom, not numbers or force, conquered.

My conclusion from this excursion through the pages
of history is that the reduction of individual choice and
competition does harm, and that their increase achieves
conditions of widening prosperity. Maximum freedom
of individual choice in economic decisions can achieve
wonders even when there is little or no freedom to vote,
as under autocratic Caesar Augustus in the early years
of the first century BC when taxes were low, trade was
free and Roman wealth expanded at an exceptional rate.

The prospect of finding a benevolent dictator who
will apply legislation designed to free the individual is
slender. Despite its shortcomings, the 'democratic' way
is our best hope of restoring choice, particularly when
ordinary voters are beginning to rebel against the
burdens of over-government and over-taxation. But the
plain warning of history is that if we do not assert the
right to choose for ourselves others will impose their
choices on us.

CHAPTER 4

Look Around
LEARNING FROM OUR OWN TIMES

To learn lessons from the history of post-war Britain, I turn first to agriculture because most of my practical experience since 1945 has been gained from farming in Sussex. That was where I developed the new 'industry' of broiler chickens in the 1950s and where I still run a modern dairy farm of 400 acres. Furthermore, agriculture is man's oldest occupation and still provides for our basic needs. Why, then, have governments tolerated and even encouraged restrictions on competition and choice which hold back efficient methods that could make food cheaper and farmers more prosperous?

AGRICULTURAL 'WELFARE'
Despite man's superior mental abilities, his main energies until recent times have had to be concentrated on producing enough to eat. So long as man has difficulties in feeding himself, he cannot turn to more advanced objectives. In countries developing most rapidly, food production has become very efficient. In this process, employment in farming has fallen which has inevitably led to economic changes that can be uncomfortable for some. Where governments plan to maximise choice, the economy will be flexible so that people will move more easily from forms of production in less demand to those in greater demand, where pay or prospects are better.

But where government claims it can solve such adjustments to change without disturbing people in their existing employments, there will naturally be ever-increasing demands on government. If the economy is not flexible, adaptation will be delayed until it becomes irresistible, and even more painful changes are necessary.

'Protection' from what?
Successive British governments have passed legislation, notably the Acts of 1947 and 1954, specifically designed to protect farmers and offer them 'assured markets'. It has been assumed that, without government aid, farmers could not stay in business and the public would not get the food it wants.

Theory confirms the lessons of experience and history that the price mechanism is a fabulous information system, cheaper and more effective even than computers. Inevitably in a world of change, it often transmits messages of changing prices and costs which the individual does not like. No one welcomes being told that his products or services are worth less or are not required: the natural response is to blame someone else or seek protection from unpleasant reality. A consequence is legislation which tries to shelter the farmer from competition or other changes. When the individual's inability to compete is due to inefficiency or changes in demand, such protection only conceals and intensifies the problem.

It is one thing to want a measure of stability or continuity, but quite another to expect to create conditions in which everyone who chooses can produce whatever he decides and stay in profitable business. Lasting stability can be achieved only by a flexible

F

price system. Who is to know what volume of production or level of prices is in the 'national interest'? Such clichés presuppose an omniscient and omnicompetent government. With the best will in the world no one can discover or decide in advance what it is in the national interest to produce, since the range of possibilities is infinite and changes all the time with new discoveries, techniques and consumer preferences.

Another favourite cliché is that government should 'provide adequate remuneration for those who live by the land'. But how can any politician or professor or, least of all, farmers' union decide what is 'fair' remuneration? Some people prefer to live in the country even though they earn less than in town. Some are highly efficient and can expand their businesses. Is this to be prevented? How can perpetual changes in methods and markets be reconciled with guaranteed 'fair' incomes or fixed prices?

As a leading poultry producer in the 1960s, I sat on a committee to advise the Minister of Agriculture on the likely future course of prices in the industry. Under the then prevailing prices and incomes policy, it was accepted that poultry was one of the products for which prices would be allowed to vary, and leading producers in their private capacity were invited to help warn the Ministry of changes. Such meetings provided minor examples of expensive procedures which, although well intentioned, waste much time and may do serious harm, especially when they lead businessmen to expect salvation from government instead of taking corrective measures to help themselves.

Thus, on one occasion, an industry 'representative' asked the Government to prevent cheap turkeys being imported from Denmark. I found it necessary to point out that, whereas a temporary ban on the importation of a few turkeys or chickens might protect the British price slightly for a short time, other regulations were already raising the costs of poultry farmers. I was referring to the minimum import prices (MIP) established for cereals with the aim of ensuring a 'reasonable' price for cereal-growers in the United Kingdom. The effect was that even if grain were available at a lower price, importers were not allowed to buy it at less than the MIP. The result was to leave an extra profit in the pockets of the foreign supplier and to raise the cost of cereals to the poultry producer so that we were paying more foreign exchange than necessary when Britain was supposed to have a balance-of-payments crisis.

The intentions were no doubt good, but they could never be achieved because the method of restricting choice must produce other consequences. As we shall see, the Common Agricultural Policy in Europe operates on similar lines and can therefore never be anything but a disaster for consumers and in the long run for many farmers.

Take eggs . . .
Successive British Governments have attempted to help egg producers in the 'obvious' way by penalising the 'rich' through taxes and market controls and giving the 'poor' a subsidy and protection from competition. Both taxes and controls represent government attempts to improve the lot of someone by reducing individual choice. The British Egg Marketing Board (BEMB), created in 1956, was a classic example of an attempt to produce a compulsory welfare situation for farmers. In 1969 the annual subsidy was £20 million which might

seem a large benefit for producers but in practice the
result was quite otherwise. At first the subsidy raised
the price received by producers but then the market
mechanism began to operate. The inevitable result was
to encourage production above the level of consumer
demand. Without a rigid system of restriction on output,
most subsidies lead to over-production which harms
instead of helping the intended beneficiary.

Some years ago I remember attending a National
Farmers' Union meeting in Uckfield, Sussex, when a
member praised the NFU for achieving an extra penny
a gallon for milk at the annual price review. In this
farmer's mind there was no awareness that an increase
in price might harm farmers by stimulating supply and
so leading to lower prices later. This example demon-
strates how people fail to grasp that price is both a
consequence and a cause. There is no such thing as a
'just' price, any more than there is a 'just' thermometer
reading. There are right prices and wrong prices. The
right price is the one that balances supply and demand
most nearly, thereby bringing stability to the market.
Stability requires flexibility, like walking a tightrope
with a balancing bar. Interfere or remove the market
mechanism and producers lack direction indicators and
lose their way. The free market is not perfect and
cannot produce complete stability; but it works towards
that end in a way no other method can do. Methods
which deny individual choice in the market must work
towards instability.

Despite large expenditures on advertising, research
and administration, the failure of the BEMB was shown
by the increasing, mostly illegal, free trade in eggs,
known as 'farm-gate' sales, which brought the producer
six old pennies more a dozen than the Board's eggs

carrying the 'lion' trade mark, plus a subsidy then running at sixpence a dozen. The culmination of a decade of well-intentioned intervention and subsidy by the Board was thus a remarkable differential between the two shillings and sixpence obtained for lion eggs and three shillings and sixpence for those sold in the free market. Something had to happen and, following an official inquiry which established the relationship between economic cause and effect, the end of both Board and subsidy was announced in January 1969, by the Minister of Agriculture in a 'socialist' government. The 'politically impossible' had happened.

Although the Board was replaced by a new Authority, the subsidy was cut from £20 million to £3 million which will not be as damaging to the industry as the old system. I certainly thought my years of almost single-handed opposition to the theory and practice of the BEMB had been well-rewarded.

Although post-war governments have attempted to interfere with the price of most farm products in addition to eggs, chicken meat production escaped because it had not developed on a sufficiently large scale when the laws were made. The result of this happy accident of timing was a rapidly growing industry which by any standards became increasingly efficient, probably the most efficient form of agricultural production, and has converted chicken from an occasional luxury dish to an everyday meal which is cheaper than other meats.

. . . and milk

The Milk Marketing Board (MMB) is more damaging than the Egg Board because it has a more complete monopoly. In the name of 'co-operative marketing', government coercion is used to fix identical retail prices throughout the country and virtually identical wholesale prices. Farmers are no longer responsible for transport costs and, however remote from their market, they are subsidised through the pooling of costs and receipts. Since 1933 when the Board was created, production has grown most rapidly where transport costs are highest. The result is to raise costs and aggravate the problem of surplus milk. By fixing prices too high, a surplus is produced which the Board tries to dispose of by a classic example of monopolistic price discrimination.

For example, in 1970 when the Board paid all farmers about 40d a gallon, it sold what it could to liquid wholesalers (i.e. for drinking as milk) at about 50d a gallon. The inevitable surplus went to manufacturers (i.e. for making into cheese, butter, powder, etc.) at about 20d a gallon. Even so, manufactured milk products had difficulty in competing with imports from distant New Zealand where summer milk fetched about 14d a gallon. For liquid milk the British housewife paid 96d a gallon compared with the 40d received by farmers.

When the MMB and the National Farmers' Union succeeded in getting import quotas against competition from foreign butter, the result was to switch New Zealand producers to cheese production against which 'voluntary' quotas were then raised. Such restrictions provide no lasting remedy. They neither discourage home production nor encourage lower costs of distribution at home. Accordingly, they provoke anguished demands from dairy farmers for domestic quotas to reduce home production and keep prices up. Thus we see how market interference designed to 'protect' farmers simply distorts production and buttresses inefficiency.

Only when the MMB is disbanded will the retail price to housewives fall to a competitive market level. Then, because production will no longer be artificially stimulated by guaranteed prices, the earnings of farmers situated in the right places will rise and more efficient organisation should make milk production into a soundly-based growth industry.[1]

... or hops

Another, lesser example of a compulsory marketing scheme is the Hops Board which has reached the ultimate monopoly position of enforcing a rigid quota system. Even at the height of the BEMB it was still possible for newcomers to start egg production, and today farmers can still enter milk production. But it is illegal for a farmer to produce hops unless he owns or buys a quota. This watertight monopoly has survived only because the annual turnover of hops is a modest £7.5 million, a tiny proportion of the total cost of beer, the price of which is inflated by massive taxes.

The Hops Board may claim it has helped growers survive against cheaper hops from abroad, but it does not know how efficient British producers would be if faced with competition and relieved of the high price for quotas, which inflates costs. Growing bananas on expensive land in greenhouses in the middle of London is manifestly absurd, but is different only in degree from giving hopgrowers a monopoly so as to keep them in production.

[1] A fuller account of the record of the MMB will be found in *The Marketing of Milk*, by Linda Whetstone, Research Monograph 21, IEA, 1970.

. . . but not chickens

Those who criticise protectionist policies must explain the workings and benefits of a market economy. For over two decades I have engaged in three forms of agricultural production: milk, chicken meat (broilers) and eggs. Only chicken production was not 'aided' by government and behind my campaign to end the Egg Board was my anxiety to stop this old restrictive philosophy being applied to the new broiler industry.

In 1953, I started with a few hundred day-old chicks. Fifteen years later the resulting company was sold for more than £20 million. Assets can thus be created with little initial capital but a lot of initiative aided by the discovery procedure of competition. The final company, Allied Farm Foods, was created from more than seventy companies with about 100 directors, of whom only five remained as directors although many others retained shareholdings. By 1968 annual sales exceeded £20 million and the value of each original Buxted £1 share had become about £550. Many investors (including me) made large sums of money in a business kept flexible by the absence of 'government protection', and a 'new' cheap food widened the choice of millions of consumers.

In the absence of well-meant government intervention, we were in direct and daily touch with our ultimate customer—the housewife—and had to bend every effort to meet her exacting requirements. Despite early criticisms about the taste of our chickens—by people who did not need to buy them—the business grew rapidly and became probably the most efficient form of agricultural production in the country. Quality improved and prices fell dramatically. I sold my first successful crop of chickens at 3s 10d a pound in 1954.

By 1968 the ex-farm price was down to 1s 7½d, which was equivalent to 7½d after allowance for inflation. Meanwhile, the company's profits had risen to £1.7 million a year.

In this pioneering form of production, where there was so much to learn about new techniques, I was often reminded of Hayek's dictum that competition is the best discovery method. We soon had computers studying eight million chickens at a time on hundreds of farms, resulting in annual sales of some 40 million birds. We experimented with many feed-stuffs and ways of controlling disease. Experience led us to see the advantages of integration both vertically and horizontally. The flow of information from hundreds of farms helped us discover the most efficient methods and the best managers. Later I achieved a similar pooling of knowledge in three dairy farms I now manage without formal integration by exchanging costings and learning both from differences and similarities. Contrary to much that is thought (and taught in schools and universities), competition does not conflict with co-operation between producers for their mutual benefit.

If freed to follow a similar course, agriculture will become more integrated and more efficient. Individual farmers will prosper by using their abilities more effectively and learning from competition about feeding, breeding and technological developments. This way of progress will be achieved if government sets about maximising choice by getting out of the way of the farmer. Innovation and progress would be assisted more by lower taxes than by higher subsidies.

No profit without risk of loss
The story of Buxted Chickens is generally considered

an outstanding business success. 'How easy to make money,' some will say. But it is not always quite so simple as it appears looking back.

When in 1968, Buxted (then known as Allied Farm Foods) was taken over, I ventured into the plastic business. It came my way as a modest-sized venture so that in the event of failure the loss would be minimised. But as I have explained, economic progress is a continuing advance into the unknown. With the plastic company, high hopes swiftly turned into unforeseen problems and eventually complete failure. It is easy with hindsight to see the mistakes I made, but that does not reduce the loss which resulted.

Another business in which I was involved from the start as an entrepreneur is concerned with the 'domestication' of the green turtle in the Caribbean. In a company established five years ago with the name 'Mariculture', my business colleagues and I have had to learn not only how to feed and maintain the turtle, which was in danger of becoming extinct, but how to get it to breed in captivity. The purpose is to produce high quality hide, oil, shell and soup products and to market them on a commercial basis despite many obstacles, made worse by the well-intentioned efforts of conservationists who seek to bring the green turtle under protection as a threatened species.

It is too early to be sure whether this venture will prove another Buxted, making large profits by supplying consumers with a competitive source of food, or another plastic bubble. Enterprise inevitably involves taking risks. Viewed in 1973, despite enormous difficulties and uncertainties aggravated by government, there is at least the possibility of an outstanding success in adding to our resources of food and other products whilst at the same time preserving the green turtle from the extinction which seemed to face it until Mariculture saw the possibility of harnessing profit and preservation.

What of Europe?

The Common Agricultural Policy (CAP) of the EEC is nothing less than a monstrous international marketing board aimed at maintaining food prices above the world level to protect inefficient French and German farmers. History enables us to predict a massive distortion of trade, high prices, vast surpluses, and consequent waste of human and physical resources (i.e. losses), leading to mounting contradictions and demands for the demolition of the entire edifice of restrictionism.

Even before the scandal of the butter mountain which was sold at a loss to Russia, surpluses of milk powder, cheese and other dairy products were piling higher despite bonuses paid for exporting them. One example of economic distortion leading to further absurdities was butter exported from the CAP countries to Yugoslavia where it was converted into mayonnaise and exported back to the EEC. The mayonnaise was then put into a centrifuge to extract vinegar and parsley and, lo and behold, butter was re-produced ready for re-export by sharp businessmen!

Other scandals have been even less honest. Since the Vatican is not within the EEC, sugar exported from Rome to the Vatican received a subsidy. This artificial barrier opened up profitable possibilities for traders. Not surprisingly, it was found that the members of the Vatican were apparently eating large quantities of sugar—some 7 lb per person per day! Similarly, large quantities of grain have moved to and fro up the EEC rivers, not being discharged but just collecting bonuses *en route*. No one should be surprised at such consequences of faking the price system by arbitrary subsidies.

High prices for producers under CAP inevitably lead to excess supplies which hang over the market and must make farmers uncertain about the future. If government would only withdraw, efficient farmers would prosper and the industry would continually be readjusting itself like any progressive industry which must take account of new demands, technical changes, consumer preferences, greater knowledge and better techniques.

Well-meant intervention once again produces damaging consequences which further distort activity in the countries to which the surpluses are exported at prices below their true costs of production. Senator Hubert Humphrey, formerly a US Presidential candidate, told a London audience in 1971 of the damage CAP has done to American agricultural markets.

'In practice CAP has become a major disruptive force in world agricultural markets. One reason is that its price levels are so far above world market levels. Another reason is that price relationships within the CAP system are set in . . . such a way as to favour the use of expensive home products in place of lower-priced imports. For example, soft wheat grown in the Common Market is increasingly used to substitute for imported corn in feeding animals . . .

Estimates by the US Department of Agriculture put the cost of the national farm support programme . . . of the European Community at

about $5,000 million a year. This must be added
to the roughly $3,000 million that is spent each
year under the CAP programme jointly managed
from Brussels. But these are not the only costs.
The high prices maintained by the CAP programme probably cost consumers in the Common
Market another $6,000 million to $7,000 million
a year over and above what they would pay if
food were available at world market prices. This
in turn releases strong inflationary forces, obliging
workers to fight for higher and higher wages to
cover their weekly food bill.'[1]

SOCIAL 'WELFARE'

Not even the most complacent apologist for politicians
would deny that the combined record of Labour and
Conservative economic and social policies since 1945 has
fallen tragically short of the high hopes of all the politicians in power during that period. What went wrong?

Post-war paradoxes

Clearly there has been no shortage of good intentions as
party men have competed with one another to promise
voters all they could possibly wish. Nor can failure be
blamed on lack of government control over the
economy. Indeed, the striking feature of public policy
since the war has been the consistency with which
politicians, irrespective of philosophy, have met almost
every problem or setback with the claim that more
taxation or more government control would put things
right. With the exception of Churchill's administration
after 1951, which 'set the people free' from the remnants

[1] Speech to the Trade Policy Research Centre, Waldorf Hotel,
London, 30 July, 1971.

of wartime restrictions with visibly beneficial results, the drift has been towards increasing control by politicians and civil servants who have taken more and more decisions away from taxpayers, consumers and businessmen. In short, the trend has been towards minimising individual choice.

Increasing taxation, mounting legislation, spreading 'welfare', sprawling subsidies, creeping—and some-times galloping—nationalisation, have led to repeated panics, particularly under the two Labour Governments which both devalued the pound (in 1949 and 1967), and have now led to an inflation without precedent in modern British history, even in time of war.

Among many bewildering paradoxes in these 28 years, three are worth calling to mind. The first is that never before have democratic politicians sought popularity with such unprincipled single-mindedness; and yet opinion polls show they have never been held in lower popular esteem. The practice of expediency has clearly proved highly inexpedient. The second is that although inflation has followed from the in-tensification of controls—over resources, location of industry, education, training, investment, prices and incomes—the only 'remedy' a Conservative Govern-ment could think of in 1972 was more of the same disastrous medicine. The third paradox is that as politicians have armed themselves with more power, they appear increasingly powerless to achieve any of their purposes. Prices rise faster, the 'floating' pound sinks, grievances multiply, and the 'welfare state' produces anything but a state of welfare.

A year before Mr Heath replaced Mr Wilson, Peregrine Worsthorne wrote of the Conservative opposition:

'At the moment, they are offering the same kind of basic prospectus as Harold Wilson offered in 1964—a change of hands on the levers controlling the domestic economy . . .'

With a short interlude of the so-called 'Selsdon Man' after their 1970 victory, the Conservatives have followed policies barely distinguishable from the choice-reducing programme of the Labour Government.

Adam Smith, again

Already by 1970, with such a large proportion of national activity outside the market, economic cause and effect were difficult enough to relate. The decision-makers no longer receive the play-back from their decisions. Those in charge of a company in a free market receive rapid reactions to their many decisions. Bad decisions swiftly produce trouble and either the policies or the man in charge are changed. In monopolistic government activities bad decisions are insulated from the self-correcting discipline of the market.

In the *Wealth of Nations*, Adam Smith foresaw the danger which he hoped might be avoided by keeping government in bounds:

'. . . though the profusion of government must, undoubtedly, have retarded the natural progress of England towards wealth and improvement, it has not been able to stop it . . . In the midst of all the exactions of government, capital has been silently and gradually accumulated by the private frugality and good conduct of individuals, by their universal, continual, and uninterrupted effort to better their own condition. It is this effort, protected by law and allowed by liberty to exert itself in the manner that is most advantageous, which has maintained the progress of England towards opulence and improvement in almost all former times and which, it is to be hoped, will do so in all future times.

England however, as it has never been blessed with a very parsimonious government, so parsimony has at no time been the characteristical virtue of its inhabitants. It is the highest impertinence and presumption, therefore, in kings and ministers, to pretend to watch over the economy of private people, and to restrain their expense, either by sumptuary laws, or by prohibiting the importation of foreign luxuries. They are themselves always, and without any exception, the greatest spendthrifts in the society.'[1]

A contemporary example of this process at work 200 years after Adam Smith wrote is provided by the nationalised industries. Between 1955 and 1970 their net income as a percentage of net assets ranged between 2.2 and 5.8 compared with the equivalent figures for private industry of 12 and 17.4. Mr George Polanyi has given the following contrast in price performance, without taking account of the many hidden subsidies to the railways and coalmines.

'Between 1951 and 1964 the average price rise of the products of the nationalised industries was 95 per cent, yet in private manufacturing industry the increase averaged only 18 per cent over the same period. Between October 1964 and March 1970 the figures were 32 per cent for nationalised products and 27 per cent for all products, so that inflation owes as much to the nationalised industries

[1] *Wealth of Nations*, Vol. I, Book II, Chap. III.

as our export success owes to private enterprise.'[1]

Mr Heath's government, like Mr Wilson's before it, now appears to believe that the one new solution to our economic problems is more technological development, which is little better than Karl Marx's assumption that work—plus large-scale 'investment'—*always* creates wealth. Hence the massive expenditures on atomic energy and Concorde, with possibly Maplin and the Channel Tunnel to follow.

Do not many of these confusions arise from the false assumption that work (or investment) necessarily creates wealth when in practice it may be misdirected and lead to losses which reduce wealth? Wealth is only the consequence of mutually advantageous voluntary exchange. If the Government sets about maximising voluntary exchange, wealth will be created at the fastest rate. If this 'maximum exchange' theory is correct, we should welcome the extension of pricing. When restrictions are applied to foreign exchanges, such as exchange control, compulsion obliterates or falsifies these indicators. The 'signposts' are then wrong and 'travellers' will take wrong turnings as surely as an aeroplane pilot will crash if he is misled by false instruments. If all road signs were turned in random directions, the more energetically travellers walked, ran or drove, the worse the muddle and the more the waste of energy. It would be no use blaming the resulting disorders on people being more lazy or less competent than elsewhere.

25p in the £

A major part of Britain's economic activity where good intentions have led to a most damaging misdirection of

---

[1] *Goodbye to Nationalisation*, Churchill Press, 1971.

G

effort and expenditure is in the so-called 'welfare state'. Before examining its inefficiency as a means of redistributing income to help the poor, let us remind ourselves that it now accounts for almost half total public expenditure and therefore about one quarter of the national income. In other words almost 25 new pennies in every £ of British income is channelled through central and local government to pay for state education, medical care, housing, pensions and other social benefits.

Let us ponder that whilst there is still no shortage of colour television sets, motor-cars, kitchen equipment, cameras or hi-fi equipment, government-provided welfare services are riddled with shortage in doctors, teachers, hospital beds, council (and rent-restricted) housing, modern schools and even state pensions sufficient for the needs of the poorest. The explanation in brief is that these welfare services are provided by state monopolies that lack the check and challenge of competing suppliers. They are financed by the public not as consumers who choose to pay prices which cover (inflated) costs, but as taxpayers who have no choice to take their money elsewhere. Choice is confined to those who are sufficiently rich to pay twice—once as conscripted taxpayers and again as paying customers for an alternative private school or health service. So we see the double damage done by state welfare services: first as monopolies which are shielded from the spur to efficiency provided by competition, and second as suppliers of 'free' or subsidised services which are therefore insulated from the test of consumer choice.

The only justification of such an inefficient, choice-denying apparatus as nationalised welfare might be if it proved a method of giving a good bargain at least to families with low incomes who might otherwise not be able to afford essential welfare services. A study of official statistics removes this last pretext from the defenders of compulsory state-financed welfare.

Who gains?
The British Central Statistical Office publishes each year in *Economic Trends* a detailed assessment of 'the incidence of taxes and social service benefits'. The figures compare the taxes paid by families of varying size and income with the estimated benefits they derive from state welfare including (where appropriate) family allowances, education, medical care, pensions and lesser benefits. The result enables us to see which families and income groups gain and which lose from the net balance between taxes paid and benefits received.

The first surprise from these published figures[1] is that even the poorest (under £9 a week) pay in taxes, on average, 25 per cent of their original incomes including cash benefits. In the income groups above £9 a week total taxes as a percentage of original income plus cash benefit vary only from 30 per cent on the lowest to 38 per cent on the highest income range. Thus over a wide range of incomes the percentages taken in taxation (including rates and social security contributions) are remarkably constant and do not show very much variation even between households with different numbers of dependants.

Table 1 shows that the average of all household incomes in unadjusted money terms rose from £18.92p per week in 1961 to £31.84p per week in 1970. This increase looks quite good until allowance is made for

[1] *Economic Trends*, February 1972.

TABLE 1

FAMILY INCOMES, TAXES AND SOCIAL BENEFITS:
  ALL HOUSEHOLDS

		£ per annum		
		1961	1965	1970 (a) (new basis)
Average incomes at current prices				
original income:	p.a.	984	1,211	1,656
	per week	18.92	23.28	31.84
income after all taxes				
and benefits:	p.a.	858	1,037	1,383
	per week	16.50	19.94	26.59
Average incomes in real terms (b)				
original income:	p.a.	984	1,051	1,150
	per week	18.92	20.21	22.13
income after all taxes				
and benefits:	p.a.	858	899	961
	per week	16.50	17.28	18.48
Estimated break-even incomes at *current prices* (c)				
after all taxes and				
benefits:	p.a.	550		950
	per week	10.57		18.26
Estimated break-even incomes in *real terms* (b) (c)				
after all taxes and				
benefits:	p.a.	550		660
	per week	10.57		12.69
Index of Retail Prices (*all items,* *monthly averages*)				
17 January 1962 = 100		97.4	112.1	140.2

(a) Before 1969 employers' contributions to national insurance and the national health service were included in original income and regarded as a direct tax; for 1969 they were excluded from original income and regarded as an indirect tax on intermediate goods and services.

(b) Figures at current prices 'deflated' by applying Index of Retail Prices (bottom line of figures above), i.e. by multiplying by 97.4 and dividing by index number for year concerned.

(c) All figures shown are very rough estimates.

Source: Department of Health and Social Security.

rising prices, when the increase in real terms is from
£18.92 to only £22.13, or barely 17 per cent over 10
years. When we turn to net income, after allowing for
taxes and benefits, we find the average increase for all
households between 1961 and 1970 was from £16.50 to
£26.59 in money terms, but from £16.50 to £18.48
after allowing for increased prices, which means that
on average *net* real incomes rose by only 12 per cent
during the decade.

TABLE 2
FAMILY INCOMES, TAXES AND SOCIAL BENEFITS:
2 ADULT, 2 CHILDREN HOUSEHOLDS

		1961	1965	1970 (a) (new basis)
Average incomes at current prices				
original income:	p.a.	1,051	1,284	1,897
	per week	20.21	24.69	36.48
income after all taxes				
and benefits:	p.a.	948	1,132	1,568
	per week	18.23	21.76	30.15
Average incomes in real terms (b)				
original income:	p.a.	1,051	1,115	1,318
	per week	20.21	21.44	25.34
income after all taxes				
and benefits:	p.a.	948	984	1,089
	per week	18.23	18.92	20.94
Estimated break-even incomes at current prices (c)				
after all taxes and				
benefits:	p.a.	650	800	1,050
	per week	12.50	15.38	20.19
Estimated break-even incomes in real terms (b) (c)				
after all taxes and				
benefits:	p.a.	650	694	729
	per week	12.50	13.34	14.01
Index of Retail Prices (all items, monthly averages)				
17 January 1962 = 100		97.4	112.1	140.2

£ per annum

Notes as for Table 1.
Source: Department of Health and Social Security.

Even more interesting are the figures shown in Table 2 for a typical family comprising a man, wife and two children. This Table also indicates the 'break-even' level of family income at which the taxes paid equal the value of welfare services received by the family. The layman who still imagines that the welfare services enjoyed by the poor are paid for by the rich is in for a large surprise. Who would guess that in 1970, when the average income for two-child families was above £36 a week, the break-even level at which the family paid as much in taxes as it got back in benefit was as low as £20? Recalling that the welfare benefits are valued at the costs incurred by inefficient state monopoly suppliers, we may surmise that on this balance-sheet of payments (taxes paid) and benefits (services received in return) even the family with a much lower than average income gets a poor bargain from the welfare state. Such a family is paying its own way in welfare, yet is denied the choice which would enable it to get better value for money from competing suppliers. It is the poorer families also which will suffer most from the resulting low rate of growth, increased inflation and high taxation which bears most heavily on low incomes.

Part of the explanation for this surprising state of affairs was given by Mr Arthur Shenfield in an essay entitled 'Trial by Taxation';[1] under the heading 'Helping the Poor?' he wrote:

> 'The redistribution of incomes has this remarkable feature, that the majority of both its champions and its opponents believe that it happens in a sense that it does not . . . The reason is that

[1] *Right Turn*, Churchill Press, 1970.

though our system does indeed tax the rich exceptionally heavily, the magnitude of the total effect is misconceived. There simply are not enough rich to make much difference . . . The modern high-taxing, high-spending state does not obtain its vast revenues from the rich but from heavy taxes on all citizens, including the poor.'

Even if we ignore the hidden inefficiency of monopoly state welfare and the effect of the resulting high taxes in inflating wage claims, it must be clear that the national balance-sheet shows a large net loss on welfare services which account for almost a quarter of total national income. Here is evidence to convince the most sceptical that the substitution of compulsion for individual choice impoverishes even those it is most intended to benefit. Its harmful effects run far wider than the inefficient provision of social welfare to the damage high taxation does to efficiency and economy.

More choice for more welfare
So far from government compulsion being necessary to ensure adequate expenditure on essential welfare services, the evidence shows that even with massive state spending, the standards in education, medical care, council housing and basic pensions are falling further behind the levels families insist on in their homes, clothing, food, holidays and personal amenities which are all supplied at competitive prices in the market. Subject to minimum requirements (like third party insurance for motorists) and government help for those in need, private provision of these welfare services would lead to more rapidly rising standards.

If consumers were free to choose between competing

welfare suppliers, they would insist on better value for their money and be prepared to pay more (voluntarily) from their own pockets than they can be induced to pay (compulsorily) in higher taxes for government services over which they have no control or choice. Some Conservative politicians like Sir Keith Joseph and Sir Geoffrey Howe used to talk as if they understood this truly humane case for choice in welfare. Experience after 1964 taught at least two leading Labour Ministers the weakness of looking to increased taxation as the way to improve welfare services.

The first was Mr Douglas Houghton whom Mr Wilson put in charge of co-ordinating Labour's social policy on pensions, health and education. Drawing on this experience, he wrote in 1967 as follows:

> 'While people would be willing to pay for better services for themselves, they may not be willing to pay more in taxes as a kind of insurance premium which may bear no relation to the services actually received.
>
> . . . from the standpoint of the quality and efficiency and the adequacy of the services, we are now getting the worst of both worlds. The government cannot find the money out of taxation and the citizen is not allowed to pay it out of his own pocket . . . there are valid objections to the state bearing out of general taxation almost the full cost of personal services which many citizens could well afford to pay for if not actually to provide for themselves.'[1]

The other Labour leader who at least glimpsed the light was Mr Richard Crossman when in 1969 he

[1] *Paying for the Social Services*, Occasional Paper 16, IEA, 1967.

launched a White Paper on national superannuation which included the following significant passage:

> '. . . people are prepared to subscribe more in a contribution for their own personal or family security then they would ever be willing to pay in taxation devoted to a wide variety of different purposes.'[1]

Who said a 'swindle'?

Perhaps a last word from two Ministers of Social Security may remove any vestige of doubt that the present system of state welfare is very different from the noble ideal which Beveridge taught the post-war generation to believe. In a book entitled *The Great Pensions 'Swindle'*,[2] Mr Arthur Seldon drew special attention to the word 'swindle' as having been used by both Labour and Conservative ministers to describe the finance of state retirement pensions. Thus in 1959 Mr Crossman, speaking for the Labour opposition, described the Conservative proposals put forward by Mr John Boyd-Carpenter as follows:

> 'I think those of us who on first reading described the White Paper as a counterfeit or bogus imitation of the Labour Party's plan were understating how bad it was. On reflection, we now realise that if we were to call this Bill a swindle we would not be exaggerating . . .'[3]

Ten years later when Mr Crossman's proposals were being debated in the House of Commons, it was Mr

---

[1] *National Superannuation and Social Insurance*, Cmnd. 3883, 1969, para. 25.

[2] Published by Tom Stacey, 1970.

[3] *Hansard*, 27 January, 1959, cols. 993–4.

Boyd-Carpenter's turn for the Conservative opposition.

> '. . . if those who were responsible for that [1959 Conservative] scheme were responsible for a swindle, it was a very small peccadillo compared with the scale of swindling operations for which the right Hon. Gentleman [Mr Crossman] is responsible.'[1]

When the political debate between leading experts on state welfare degenerates into a question of how big a swindle its financing really is, the case for radical reform to restore individual choice surely becomes irresistible. A reduction in universal subsidies would increase choice, first, for the better-off majority by reducing taxation and, second, for the really poor minority by more generous assistance, perhaps in the form of vouchers.[2]

GOVERNMENT SPENDING AND INFLATION

Although state welfare is the largest area over which individual choice is more or less suppressed by centralised political decision, all taxation is a denial of voluntary exchange between willing buyer and willing seller where both gain from the transaction. Some idea of the reduction in choice from this source is conveyed by the proportion of total national income spent by central and local government; although there are more ways than one of measuring such magnitudes and inflation quickly renders any monetary totals out of date.

From the *Financial Statement* published by Mr

---

[1] *Hansard*, 6 March, 1969, cols. 742–3.

[2] Possible reforms are set out in *Down with the Poor*, Churchill Press, 1971, and discussed in more detail in Chapter 6 below.

Anthony Barber when he introduced his Budget in
March 1973, we can work out that total public
expenditure planned for 1973–4 was about £32,000
million while all forms of taxation amounted to about
£27,600 million, leaving a deficit (described by the
Treasury as the 'borrowing requirement') of £4,400
million. If we put the total national income in present
money values at around £55,000 million, we can see
that public spending accounts for well over half of all
spending. The result is not only high taxation which
reduces individual choice, but also the piling up of
pressures which make for inflation.

In 1945 Dr Colin Clark concluded from extensive
study that where taxation (plus government deficits)
exceeded 25 per cent of the national income,

> 'then forces were set in motion which resulted, not
> immediately but within two or three years, in a
> general rise in costs and prices.'[1]

Almost 20 years later he brought his researches up to
date and found that countries with the best record on
inflation (then including Japan and Switzerland) had
kept taxes below his critical level of 25 per cent. Dr
Clark's general explanation of the cause-and-effect link
between high taxes and rising prices was as follows:

> '. . . taxation raises costs partly through discourag-
> ing productive effort; more significantly, perhaps,
> in causing industrialists to become careless about
> costs (if half of any increase in costs is "on the
> Treasury", they will make much less effort to

[1] The original findings were published in *Economic Journal*,
December 1945; the words quoted are from Colin Clark's
Taxmanship, Hobart Paper 26, IEA, 1964.

avoid it, whether it be a wage increase, interest charges, or an expense account) and, finally and in rather a subtle manner, the existence of a high level of taxation alters the whole climate of politics: politicians tend to lose their capacity to resist pressures, whether governmental or private, leading to cost increases, in the more or less unconscious knowledge that a rise in prices will lower the real value of all fixed charges on the budget and in that way lighten their burden.'[1]

Since Colin Clark wrote these words, the record of Labour and Conservative Governments on Concorde, and Mr Heath's subsequent commitment to the Maplin project, almost exactly illustrate this irresponsible attitude towards costly gambles on the scale of £1,000 million each. If high taxation leads to carelessness in public and private spending, it follows that the poor value for money received by government has the effect of diluting its value.

It is interesting that a similar finding has been reached by Mr Ronald Burgess working independently on accountancy lines at the Economic Study Association. In November 1971, he wrote:

'My own work on local government finance has led me to the conclusion that in any given situation there is a definite limit to public income and that public expenditure must be adjusted to this limit.'[2]

Money and the unions
Mr Heath has maintained that the cause of inflation

---

[1] *Ibid.*, pp. 23–24.
[2] *Local Government Finance*, Paper No. 2, Economic Study Association, 1971.

lies in the power of trade unions to enforce excessive wage demands. Certainly the trade unions have too much power, but if government did not prop up public and private 'lame ducks', spend vast sums of taxpayers' money uneconomically, and stifle competition in all its forms, the trade unions would have less scope to inflate money wages and more prospects of increased real wages. At present the impact of marginal tax rates on 'take-home pay' means that wage increases of perhaps 12 or 14 per cent are needed to offset an increase in prices of 10 per cent.

Certainly legislation is necessary to make unions subject to contract and put an end to intimidation and compulsion, but the most logical reason for not blaming inflation on them has been stated by Professor Milton Friedman who has summarised[1] much historical research as follows:

> 'It is easy to show that the widely held union-wage-push theory of inflation is not correct. If A is *the* cause of B, then whenever A occurs, B will also occur, and whenever B occurs, so will A. *Trade unions* (A) were as strong in the US in 1961–64, when there was no *inflation* (B), as in 1965–69, when there was inflation. Prices in the US more than doubled in the Civil War, when unions were almost non-existent, in World War I, when unions were weak, and in World War II when unions were strong. Prices in the US rose more than 30 per cent from 1849 to 1857, and again from 1895 to 1914, both periods when unions were extremely weak.

[1] 'Inflation and Wages', in *An Economist's Protest*, Thomas Horton, New Jersey, 1973.

Inflation has plagued countries with negligible trade unions and with strong trade unions; and both kinds of countries have had periods of price stability. Communist countries, like capitalist countries, have experienced both inflation and price stability . . .'

So we return to Colin Clark's central finding. But if excessive taxation creates conditions that favour a general rise in costs and prices, this effect can be sustained over a period only if governments obligingly increase the circulation of money to finance a similar volume of transactions at higher monetary values.

Friedman, who places primary blame for inflation on lax monetary policy, and Colin Clark who blames taxation, strongly reinforce each other when we look at British public finances. From the figures mentioned earlier it will be recalled that despite a record level of taxation in the current year, the Chancellor of the Exchequer is running a deficit of over £4,000 million to catch up with a runaway expenditure of £32,000 million. Both Friedman[2] and Clark would agree that the financing of this deficit with the help of the printing press and newly-created credit must lead to inflation. So long as monetary inflation is being stoked up, no prices and incomes policy can stop the effect working its way through, first into the uncontrolled sector of foodstuffs, land, housing, gold, antiques, and then throughout the economy as the controls are relaxed or evaded or completely overwhelmed by the pent-up pressure of monetary demand.

More than 15 years ago a private banker with

[2] *The Counter-Revolution in Monetary Theory*, Occasional Paper 33, IEA, 1970.

first-hand experience of the great German inflation of
1923 warned British politicians that they were heading,
however gradually, in precisely the same direction. In
his forthright evidence to the Radcliffe Commission on
money and credit (1957),[1] Mr Walter Salomon summarised the central cause and main cures of inflation
as follows:

> 'Inflation has persisted for 12 years after the end
> of the war primarily because the state plays too
> large a part in economic activity. This has made
> the supply of money larger than it should have
> been and the output of goods and services smaller
> than it could have been. The solutions lie in
> reducing public expenditure, tightening control
> over the supply of money and credit, reducing
> taxation, offering stronger incentives to effort and
> saving, and revitalising industry by re-asserting
> the authority of the owners and restoring com-
> petition.'

Where Mr Salomon says the state 'plays too large a
part', I have expressed much the same thing in
criticising policies that minimise private choice. If he
and the academics I have quoted here agree that
this centralisation of decisions is the basic source also
of inflation, then here is another devil we may hope to
exorcise by restoring choice (along with a large part
of taxation) back to the individual who will insist on
better value in spending his own money.

Voluntary exchange benefits all
Starting from first principles, and checking the result

[1] Reproduced with other essays in *One Man's View*, Churchill
Press, 1973.

against history and practical experience, I have suggested that wealth is created when voluntary exchange is maximised. I must repeat that this does not mean 'no laws' or inactive government. On the contrary, it means government by general rules. White lines, yellow lines, traffic lights, highway codes restrict the use of roads for everyone. This requires legislation which deliberately aims to ensure maximum freedom for motorists to use roads effectively, without ignoring the claims of pedestrians.

If wealth is created at the fastest rate when voluntary exchanges are at a maximum, it must follow that wealth will be at a minimum when exchanges do not exist. Exchanges will take place when bargaining over price is voluntary, even between two people living on an island. Only restrictive legislation can prevent exchanges completely, though it usually fails. As we would expect, even under the most severe prohibitions, private voluntary exchanges break through in what are called 'black (or grey) markets'.

If we follow the logic, we can equate benefits with voluntary exchange, and lack of benefits (or losses) with its absence. A benefit is the margin of satisfaction each party to a transaction derives from exchanging something he values less for something he values more. In voluntary exchange both sides benefit. Economists describe this little understood fact briefly as 'gains from trade'. It holds the secret of a prosperous, free and stable society. The opposite way of government restriction and compulsion leads to a lesser benefit or loss. Might inflation at rock bottom be caused by the government's effort to make good this loss by creating money?

Compulsion reduces satisfaction

Some people may still find it difficult to understand my central argument in this book. If two people willingly exchange something for something else we may suppose, in a society of reasonable people, that both think they are doing well out of the deal. This is as true of schoolboys swapping conkers for a cricket card of Colin Cowdrey or Gary Sobers as it is for a man exchanging money for a commodity or a service. Of course, we should make it easier for them to know what they are exchanging by providing information and punishing false claims, but the general argument is that by exchanging goods or services freely, and receiving something they value more in return for what they give, people *increase* the total value of *all* the goods and services available as a whole.

It must also follow, of course, that people who are *forced* to exchange do not benefit in the same way. The assumption is that if they had stood to gain they would not have needed to be forced to exchange. And compulsory exchange includes the payment of taxation (or local rates or national insurance contributions) for the services supplied by central or local government. All one can say is that they are likely to be valued less, and probably much less, than the money they have had taken away from them in taxes. Compulsion must reduce the satisfaction individuals derive from their incomes.

In other words, the vast amount of money spent on so-called 'public services', and on government itself, may be worth much less than the value on paper shown in terms of pounds. Yet 'public expenditure' is included in the national income as though it were worth as much as the values created by voluntary exchange.

H

There could be no greater fallacy. A pound spent by a civil servant does *not* add as much value as a pound spent by a person backing his own judgement and 'bettering his condition'. Government may be, for some activities, a necessary evil; but it is a bad substitute for voluntary exchange wherever free markets can be allowed to function.

Hope from Indonesia

From an abundance of evidence, let me conclude with an unexpected example of the practical application of my principle about maximising choice from Indonesia. It will be found in an official publication of the International Monetary Fund (IMF).[1] After years of communist dictatorship in Indonesia, inflation speeded up in the early 1960s until by mid-1966 prices were rising at an annual rate of more than 1,500 per cent. The communists were overthrown in a bloody revolution and by October 1966 the new Government was ready to launch a very different policy based essentially on freeing individual choice from communist-style controls.

The following record is an abbreviated account which relies as far as possible on the words used in the IMF report to describe the principles pursued and their consequences. The basic change was 'away from a government-dominated economy towards a system in which market forces played a predominant role'. This new approach led the government to 'curtail less essential budget expenditures and to eliminate the large operational losses of many public sector enterprises'. Abroad came the introduction of 'an exchange system virtually free of restrictions on payments, with

[1] *Finance and Development*, IMF Quarterly, No. 4, 1970.

flexible exchange rates for most transactions'. The budget was balanced by 1968 and a firmer grip was taken on monetary policy. From 760 per cent in 1966, the rate of increase in the money supply fell to 120 per cent in 1968 and 60 per cent in 1969. Where stabilisation was expected to take many years, the remarkable consequences of this about-face in policy were seen by 1969 when the rate of inflation had fallen from 1,500 to 10 per cent.

Did the result support what the IMF report calls 'the popular belief that stabilisation needs to entail economic stagnation or recession'? This is how the question was answered in its own words:

> 'Although comprehensive statistics are not available, import and export data as well as other indicators strongly suggest that the stabilisation period was marked by a substantial increase in economic activity . . .
>
> Provided that available resources are allocated primarily on the basis of economic criteria, stabilisation can indeed proceed simultaneously with economic growth.'

No wonder the report concludes that 'the Indonesian programme represents a promising model of anti-inflationary policies'.

Warning from the Common Market
We have already glimpsed some of the absurdities of the EEC as it restricts choice for producers and consumers in agriculture. Whatever the theory or wider hopes for British membership of the EEC, one of the Commissioners, Dr Ralf Dahrendorf, has warned

of the reality. In *The Times*[1] he was reported as saying that the Commission has become

> '. . . an illiberal and bureaucratic leviathan obsessed with harmonising things just for the sake of harmonisation . . .'

For hundreds of years an Englishman has been considered innocent until proved guilty and still enjoys freedom to appeal to higher courts. In Brussels the only court to which an Englishman accused by the Commission of breaking one of the countless proliferating regulations may appeal is the European Court of Justice. Sir Henry Slessor (a former Labour Solicitor General) wrote to *The Times*,[2] warning that European justice is not the same as British justice:

> 'As a Lord Justice of Appeal (retired) and a member of the Judicial Committee of the Privy Council I venture to call the attention of your readers to a fact which, in my view, differentiates the United Kingdom in a very essential matter from the whole Continent.
>
> The laws of England, those of the United States, the Dominions and those now independent Afro-Asian states (the last through the education of their leaders and the universal decisions of the Privy Council) were and are based on the libertarian principles of the Common Law.
>
> In contrast the European system of Roman Law is based on the didactic codified edicts of authority, derived from Justinian and Napoleon.
>
> This is not merely a juristic difference but also a fundamental divergence of outlook; the one

[1] 2 August, 1971.
[2] 16 July, 1971.

favouring freedom, and the other emphasising authority.

England has never been a part of Europe since the departure of the Romans; even Charlemagne did not include England in the Holy Roman Empire.'

In *The Daily Telegraph*[1] a month later, Ronald Bell, MP, QC, commented:

'This Treaty of 248 Articles is abstract, jealous, pedantic, and more pervasive than is commonly realised. There is little that does not come within the range of ensuring fair competition, even recipes for beer, wine and sauces, the shape of bottles, working hours and conditions. Brussels has the power to rule almost all except defence and foreign policy, and within about five years will be largely doing so . . .'

Without realising it the British public have been led along a path which must lead even more rapidly to less choice. The giving up of Magna Carta and the Bill of Rights are major issues and not just the tearing up of 'scraps of paper'. How does all this come about? As always when choice is minimised, it happen 'slowly, slowly' without the victims realising the implications.

In his *Anatomy of Britain*,[2] Anthony Sampson gives his judgement:

'. . . the most drastic by-pass of Parliament has been the most important of all post-war issues—the question of joining the Common Market. When the Treaty of Rome was prepared in 1957, none of the European Parliaments was able to discuss it in

[1] 17 August, 1971.
[2] Hodder & Stoughton, London, 1962.

detail: the Treaty itself had been drafted by delegates from each country, who spent several months with their civil servants, negotiating and working out the complicated technical questions of tariffs, capital movement, agriculture. The Treaty was then put forward to the Parliaments virtually as a *fait accompli*, to be either rejected or ratified as a whole. The arrangements were far too technical to be left to ordinary Parliamentarians: faced with a take-it-or-leave-it proposition, they reluctantly took it.'

The dangers were emphasised by Oxford economist Peter Oppenheimer when he took a forward look at the Commission's efforts to achieve 'harmonisation':

'In technical matters harmonisation is unobjectionable but the Commission will not stop here. In the long run it is bound to turn its attention to such areas as professional qualifications and recruitment methods, organisation of public services, school and university structure and a host of other matters. Where others see the cultural diversity of Europe, the Common Market Commission sees only distortions in the labour market and unfair competitive advantage.

"Harmonising" Europe will mean destroying much of this cultural diversity and transforming the Continent into a bureaucratic parade-ground. How ironic if the gentlemen in Brussels are able to destroy in the next generation what Soviet tanks on one side and coca cola on the other have allowed to escape in our own day!'[1]

[1] 'Europe and the Common Market', in the *National Westminster Bank Review*, February 1971.

A last warning

Since the United States economy is the largest and the most successful so far evolved by man, much can be learned from American experience. The key lesson is that past success has not prevented the syndrome from appearing. The incredible wealth of the USA after the Second World War made it seem that their riches were unlimited and they could do what they liked. One consequence was ever-increasing government expenditure, some of it in a bewildered endeavour to put most of the rest of the world onto a sound economic footing by one form of subsidy or another. Added to this expenditure was the burden of the Vietnam War and mounting extravagance on the 'great society' programmes, in a vain effort to hasten the millennium.

Such over-spending could have been expected to produce inflationary consequences, including balance-of-payments deficits, and it promptly did. By 1969 it could be foreseen that even a Republican Administration would endeavour to 'hold' prices and wages with controls. At the end of 1970 President Nixon was pleading with business and labour to try to restrain price increases and wage demands while pumping more money into the economy. King Canute would have known better.

About this time Professor Milton Friedman visited London and was interviewed by the *Sunday Times*.[1] Asked if the impression was correct that he regarded inflation as the greatest economic evil, he replied:

'No. Inflation *per se* is not a good thing but it is not the greatest economic evil. The greatest economic evil arises out of the measures that are mistakenly

[1] 20 September, 1970.

used to combat inflation like pegging exchange rates and seeking to influence wages and prices through incomes policies, freezes and other forms of control . . . if you have open inflation it is perfectly possible for people to adjust to it. They will come to expect it. Interest rates will go up, wages will escalate. The market can operate to enable individuals through private transactions to allocate resources and organise economic activity.

On the other hand, if you repress price movements, if you hold particular prices or wages fixed, you destroy the market mechanism. You must have something in its place. What gets put in its place is either chance, favouritism, bribery or governmental control. We have ample experience that these methods are highly inefficient. May I say also that the pretended cures are not cures. I know of no inflation at any time, anywhere, which has ever been cured by wage or price control or freeze.'

Must Diocletian's lesson be learned again by bitter experience, 'after much blood shed on trifling account'?

CHAPTER 5

What Can be Done
EXAMPLES OF THEORY IN ACTION

The main threads of my argument have been that individuals are not powerless victims of fate; that history proves we can do something to avert recurrent disaster; and that if we act with understanding of natural forces or principles, the improvement in our economic fortunes could be dramatic and sustained. Against the background of a dangerous drift to disaster in the post-war years, I now want to set out some of my experience over this period that may encourage rational hopes for the future.

At the end of the war I was very troubled about whether the deaths and other sacrifices would once again fail to bring the freedom, prosperity and lasting peace for which we were told we had fought. The omens of the 1945 General Election did not strike me as too promising. What I would now call the minimising of individual choice by the Labour Government made me even more pessimistic about the direction party politics seemed to be taking us.

Birth of the IEA
About this time, I read a shortened version[1] of Professor Hayek's *Road to Serfdom* and was so impressed that I bought the book and sought out the author. It was for me a fateful meeting. My central question was what, if anything, he could advise me to do to help get

[1] *Reader's Digest*, May 1945.

discussion and policy on the right lines. I do not recall his exact words but have retained almost 30 years later a vivid impression of his message. Hayek first warned against wasting time—as I was then tempted—by taking up a political career. He explained his view that the decisive influence in the great battle of ideas and policy was wielded by the intellectuals whom he characterised as the 'second-hand dealers in ideas'.[1] It was the dominant intellectuals from the Fabians onward who had tilted the political debate in favour of growing government intervention with all that followed. If I shared the view that better ideas were not getting a fair hearing, his counsel was that I should join with others in forming a scholarly research organisation to supply intellectuals in universities, schools, journalism and broadcasting with authoritative studies of the economic theory of markets and its application to practical affairs.

Two years later I heard a lecture by Mr Ralph Harris who had just come down from Cambridge with a first in economics and who seemed to share precisely my doubts about the dominant intellectual climate of opinion. I introduced myself and we took each other's name and address. In 1953 I started my chicken business and by 1955 felt sufficiently hopeful of the financial prospects to form an educational trust with the title Institute of Economic Affairs (IEA).

A footnote in *The Road to Serfdom*[2] on exchange controls inspired the first venture into publication of the embryonic IEA.

---

[1] 'The Intellectuals and Socialism', *University of Chicago Law Review*, Spring 1949 (reprinted in *Studies in Philosophy, Politics and Economics*, Routledge and Kegan Paul, 1967).

[2] Routledge, 1944, p. 69.

'The extent of the control over all life that economic control confers is nowhere better illustrated than in the field of foreign exchanges. Nothing would at first seem to affect private life less than a state control of the dealings in foreign exchange, and most people will regard its introduction with complete indifference. Yet the experience of most continental countries has taught thoughtful people to regard this step as the decisive advance on the path to totalitarianism and the suppression of individual liberty.

It is in fact the complete delivery of the individual to the tyranny of the state, the final suppression of all means of escape—not merely for the rich, but for everybody. Once the individual is no longer free to travel, no longer free to buy foreign books or journals, once all the means of foreign contact can be restricted to those of whom official opinion approves or for whom it is regarded as necessary, the effective control of opinion is much greater than that ever exercised by any of the absolutist governments of the seventeenth and eighteenth centuries.'

As an experiment, I commissioned a free-lance economic journalist, Mr George Winder, to write *The Free Convertibility of Sterling*. It was published by Batchworth Press in 1956 at the cost of £200 for 2,000 copies. The first intellectual to respond was Henry Hazlitt who devoted his regular column in *Newsweek* to an enthusiastic review. Orders came in from around the world and over the following years I was to meet many readers of George Winder's little classic as evidence of Hayek's process of long-term education at work.

Thus encouraged, I got in touch with Ralph Harris who by 1956, at the age of 31, had finished seven years teaching at St. Andrews University and had moved to the *Glasgow Herald* as a leader writer. In January 1957, on the promise of £1,000 in the bank, he agreed to come to London as 'General Director' (and sole employee) of the Institute of Economic Affairs in a small city office rented for £3 a week. At last there was the beginning of what might now be called a 'think tank' with the difference that it was as independent of politics as of business or any other interest. Helped by an Advisory Council which included Sir Oscar Hobson, Colin Clark, Professor Eric Nash, Graham Hutton and George Schwartz, its purpose was set out in early publications as being:

> '. . . to foster public understanding of how economic principles can illumine the great public issues of the day and in particular to examine economic policies by reference to the requirements of a free society.'

Among its early publications were studies of pensions, trade unions, advertising, hire purchase, the City's earnings, the sterling problem and monetary policy which certainly had consequences at the intellectual level though they taught lessons for policy that have still not been fully learned 15 years later. The first author Ralph Harris commissioned was another first-class economist, LSE-trained Arthur Seldon, who after writing *Pensions in a Free Society* promptly joined the IEA in 1958 and has ever since been its Editorial Director. In 1959 they recruited two secretaries and moved to a basement office at Hobart Place which gave its name to the IEA's most famous series, the *Hobart Papers*.

Call for freedom

Meanwhile, I had drawn further encouragement from an international group of scholars, writers and more thoughtful businessmen which also owed its inspiration to Professor Hayek. In April 1947, he had invited leading liberal economists and philosophers to a private conference at Mont Pelerin, near Vevey in Switzerland, from which has grown the Mont Pelerin Society (MPS). Its aim as drafted by Hayek and approved by those attending that first meeting, may be worth quoting in full for reflection more than 25 years later.

'A group of economists, historians, philosophers and other students of public affairs from Europe and the United States met at Mont Pelerin, Switzerland, from April 1st to 10th, 1947, to discuss the crisis of our times. This group, being desirous of perpetuating its existence for promoting further intercourse and for inviting the collaboration of other like-minded persons, has agreed upon the following statement of aims.

The central values of civilisation are in danger. Over large stretches of the earth's surface the essential conditions of human dignity and freedom have already disappeared. In others they are under constant menace from the development of current tendencies of policy.

The position of the individual and the voluntary group are progressively undermined by extensions of arbitrary power. Even that most precious possession of Western Man, freedom of thought and expression, is threatened by the spread of creeds which, claiming the privilege of tolerance when in the position of a minority, seek only to establish a position of power in which they can suppress and obliterate all views but their own.

The group holds that these developments have been fostered by the growth of a view of history which denies all absolute moral standards and by the growth of theories which question the desirability of the rule of law. It holds further that they have been fostered by a decline of belief in private property and the competitive market; for without the diffused power and initiative associated with these institutions, it is difficult to imagine a society in which freedom may be effectively preserved.

Believing that what is essentially an ideological movement must be met by intellectual argument and the reassertion of valid ideals, the group, having made a preliminary exploration of the ground, is of the opinion that further study is desirable *inter alia* in regard to the following matters:

(1) the analysis and explanation of the nature of the present crisis so as to bring home to others its essential moral and economic origins;

(2) the redefinition of the functions of the state so as to distinguish more clearly between the totalitarian and the liberal order;

(3) methods of re-establishing the rule of law and of assuring its development in such manner that individuals and groups are not in a position to encroach upon the freedom of others, and private rights are not allowed to become a basis of predatory power;

(4) the possibility of establishing minimum standards by means not inimical to initiative and the functioning of the market;

(5) methods of combating the misuse of history for the furtherance of creeds hostile to liberty;

(6) the problem of the creation of an international order conducive to the safeguarding of peace and liberty and permitting the establishment of harmonious international economic relations.

The group does not aspire to conduct propaganda. It seeks to establish no meticulous and hampering orthodoxy. It aligns itself with no particular party. Its object is solely, by facilitating the exchange of views among minds inspired by certain ideals and broad conceptions held in common, to contribute to the preservation and improvement of the free society.'

In 1959 Ralph Harris helped organise the 10th International Conference of the MPS at Oxford where leading British economists associated with the IEA (including Graham Hutton, John Jewkes, Herbert Frankel, Basil Yamey, Peter Bauer, S. R. Dennison) were able to renew links that were to bear much fruit with such outstanding European and American scholars as Wilhelm Röpke, Milton Friedman, George Stigler, Ludwig Erhard, Fritz Machlup, Karl Brandt, James Buchanan, Gottfried Haberler, Trygve Hoff, W. H. Hutt, Frank Knight, and Jacques Rueff.

The case of rpm . . .
In January 1960, the Institute published its first Hobart Paper, a critical study of resale price maintenance (rpm) by Professor B. S. Yamey. I recall

asking Ralph Harris why he thought a study of such an apparently dull, little-noticed subject was worth producing. I have never forgotten his answer which was that the argument was 'so well documented, scholarly and convincing'. With hindsight, it is easy to understand why rpm had not previously been dealt with, either by a trade association, trade union or political party. It was a restrictive practice designed to help sellers by confining consumer choice to fixed prices for branded products. Only a completely independent organisation could risk offending such a powerful lobby as the small shopkeepers, who traditionally had come to think of rpm as a protection against more efficient forms of retailing.

Four years later Mr Edward Heath, who as President of the Board of Trade was piloting a Bill through the House of Commons to end rpm, lunched at the Institute and met Basil Yamey. He pointed to him, saying 'You are the cause of all my trouble'. The 'trouble' was the political fracas in his own party as well as from Labour MPs, trade associations and some manufacturers who felt threatened by the restoration of competitive prices. It may have been politically inexpedient to take this action a few months before the 1964 Election, but it certainly contributed to the reforming reputation of Mr Heath which propelled him into the leadership of the Tory Party the following year.

Here was a classic example of an intellectual working away in a 'backroom' without any political power, ambition or intent, having a practical effect through attracting the attention of reviewers, civil servants and finally men of action. Subsequently, a mutual friend who knew Mr Heath well told me how he tried to get

Mr Heath at the Board of Trade to tackle another
pressing problem but Mr Heath explained that, having
the choice between two reforms, he went for rpm
because the case was fully documented. Here was
tangible proof of Hayek's view that scholarly research
should take pride of place over political campaigning.

The success of Hobart Paper 1 as a student text was
proved by the publication of four editions within as
many years after its first appearance.

Over the centuries it has been the scholar who
applied most thought to his subject who has best
understood it. He is thus able to produce a well-
reasoned and documented thesis which can achieve the
greatest consequences. He himself is most unlikely ever
to take any form of political action, both because this
will prevent the desired consequence and probably also
because, living in the academic world, he will not have
political ambitions. Right or wrong, he may have been
dead for many years before his work has consequences.

A frequent criticism of the IEA approach to education is that its publications do not reach the 'masses'.
But they are aimed at a different 'market', namely
Hayek's 'intellectuals', who as teachers and writers
retail ideas for wider consumption. Their strength is
based on the belief that the scholar who understands
his subject best and can convince his peers, will have
the most effect, though it will often take longer than
four years to win through.

. . . and nuclear energy
It has been the experience of the IEA that when a
study is authoritative, logical, clearly written and
avoids political partisanship, it will attract attention
in press, radio and television and will be noticed

I

by civil servants and MPs of all political 'colours'.

Since 1957 the IEA has published works by about 200 authors of diverse political allegiances and of none, on aspects of market pricing and competition in a wide range of goods and services, whether supplied by private or public enterprise, including welfare, roads, telephones, postal services, currencies and savings. An important example was Research Monograph 9, *The Political Economy of Nuclear Energy*, written by an independent economic consultant, Professor Duncan Burn. The disappointing result of nuclear power in Britain controlled by the monopolistic Atomic Energy Authority was contrasted with the success of the US Atomic Energy Commission which from the start encouraged competition and private enterprise. The original mistake was traced back to 1941 when expert scientists advised the government that such an important potential must 'not be allowed to fall into the hands of private business'. From this restriction of choice followed the sorry story summarised in a half-page review in the *Daily Mirror*[1] which lamented: 'Britain no longer leads the world in putting the atom to work'.[2]

By an interesting coincidence, whilst lecturing in the USA, I met in Dallas, Texas, the man responsible for American atomic energy policy. He was an attorney who on returning after the war decided that it was dangerous for government to have a monopoly of nuclear power and set about doing something about it.

[1] 1 May, 1967.
[2] The latest development in this sorry story was a report in the *Daily Telegraph* (1 November, 1973) that the Government is being urged by the CEGB to allow American nuclear power plants (based on the light water reactor) to be built in Britain. The proposal was described as 'a move which could kill the British nuclear development programme.'

Naturally, I was interested and requested more information. Working as a private citizen, he prepared plans to balance private initiative with the necessary framework of government control. Over a period of ten years, Congress enacted a number of laws culminating in an Act permitting the private ownership of nuclear materials in the same manner as gas, oil, and coal. In retrospect, this creative process blossomed due to one individual—a private, non-political person—acting early in a well thought-out manner to preserve the 'discovery procedure' of competition on the grounds that no government agency can produce an Einstein.

The lesson we can learn is that laws being passed today have their origins many years ago. My story illustrates that, to be effective, determined effort must be aimed toward the often distant future because, once a pattern is set, it requires even greater effort to reverse the trend. The mills of government grind slowly, but an essential factor in seeing they grind well is the challenge of free and educated citizens.

Few stories more clearly demonstrate the power of individuals prepared to think out policies from first principles without being diverted by political considerations or conventional talk of the right course being 'politically impossible'.

The Hobart Papers

Ten years after Professor Yamey's classic, IEA published the fiftieth Hobart Paper.[1] To mark this milestone, Arthur Seldon invited Professor T. W. Hutchison, an independent authority on the development of economic thought and policy, to appraise the contri-

[1] Dr Brian Hindley, *Industrial Merger and Public Policy*, IEA, 1970.

bution which the series had made 'to a better understanding of the role of economic analysis in fashioning
and criticising public and business policy'. In the
resulting *Half a Century of Hobarts*, published in 1970,
Professor Hutchison commended the series as per-
forming

> '. . . the valuable service of keeping alive, against
> a tide of much influential current opinion, theories
> and ideas of great relevance for policy which had
> been temporarily submerged in this country not
> by any weight of empirical evidence and testing,
> but rather by dogmatism, fashion and ideology.'

On their quality he concluded:

> 'It is fortunate for the enlightened discussion of
> economic policies . . . that at least from one
> direction . . . proposals are being put forward in
> terms of economic analysis and predictions of the
> technical quality, range, carefulness, consistency
> and rigour generally shown in the *Hobart Papers*.'

On their distinctive approach, he wrote:

> '. . . the main thrust of the Hobart attack consists
> in advocating and advancing the use of pricing
> and market mechanisms and competitive forces,
> based on an underlying philosophy which starts
> from a strong preference for the decentralisation
> of initiative, and for the revival or extension of
> freedom of choice for individuals as buyers and
> sellers . . .'

Finally, on the impact of the Hobart contribution to
public discussion of competitive enterprise, Professor
Hutchison quoted a testimony from the opposing camp:

'. . . perhaps it is sufficient to point out that "even the ranks of Tuscany"—or the Fabian Society—have "scarce foreborn to cheer". In a recent Fabian tract[1] it has been maintained that the Hobart series (and other IEA publications) "must be respected for the quality, consistency and rigour of its approach to the treatment of private industry . . . This is very far removed from a crude approach based on the vested interests of capitalists . . . Its careful description of, and attacks upon, restrictive trade practices has been particularly impressive . . . I concede a consistent and honourable attempt to remove a major blemish of the free market system".'

The importance of such long-term educational efforts is that politicians and those who advise them have no time in office to think ahead in a coherent, much less objective way. Their dilemma has been described by Mr Enoch Powell with characteristic force and wit:

'The supreme function of statesmanship is to provide against preventable evils. In seeking to do so, it encounters obstacles which are deeply rooted in human nature. One is that by the very order of things such evils are not demonstrable until they have occurred; and at each stage in their onset there is room for doubt and for dispute whether they be real or imaginary.

By the same token they attract little attention in comparison with current troubles, which are both indisputable and pressing: whence the besetting temptation of all politics to concern itself with the

[1] David Collard, *The New Right: A critique*, Fabian Society, 1968.

immediate present at the expense of the future. Above all, people are disposed to mistake predicting troubles for causing troubles and even for desiring troubles. "If only", they love to think. "If only people wouldn't talk about it, it probably wouldn't happen." Perhaps this habit goes back to the primitive belief that the word and the thing, the name and the object, are identical.

At all events the discussion of future grave but, with effort now, avoidable evils is the most unpopular and at the same time most necessary occupation for the politician. Those who knowingly shirk it deserve and not infrequently receive the curses of those who come after.'[1]

For approaching two decades the IEA so far from shirking the discussion of 'future grave but avoidable evils' has encouraged its authors to follow their argument wheresoever it leads them. The results have been such that no conscientious reader of IEA publications would be taken by surprise by the recurrent signs of the following 'avoidable evils': the failure of the welfare state,[2] the collapse of the market for houses to rent,[3] the 'land racket',[4] road congestion,[5] the ineffectiveness of incomes policies,[6] the damaging aspects of EEC membership,[7] the misuses of trade union

[1] Speech to West Midlands Area Conservative Political Centre, Birmingham, 20 April, 1968.

[2] Harris and Seldon, *Choice in Welfare 1963*, and many other reports.

[3] Norman Macrae, *To Let*, 1960.

[4] Professor Donald Denman, *Land in the Market*, 1967.

[5] Gabriel Roth, *A Self-financing Road System*, 1966.

[6] Professor F. W. Paish, *Policy for Incomes*, 1964.

[7] Professor J. E. Meade, *UK, Commonwealth and Common Market*, 1962.

power,[1] the danger of a monetary explosion,[2] the co-existence of a record level of unemployment with an unprecedented rate of inflation.[3]

An independent university?
A last example of the effectiveness of the IEA's unique pioneering approach is provided by its publication in 1969 of an Occasional Paper entitled *Towards an Independent University* by Professor H. S. Ferns, a former socialist who had become disillusioned by the spread of state control, first in the Argentine under President Peron and then in Britain under Mr Wilson. As the judgement of a political scientist, his opening paragraph commands special attention.

'For nearly three-quarters of a century more and more people of all classes and occupations have become more and more dependent in one way or another upon the state and have accordingly come under its control. It is now becoming increasingly obvious that this dependence and control are doing the community more harm than good, and that the moral and social energy of the people is diminishing through undue and prolonged entanglements in the web of government.

The time has come to demonstrate on a large scale and in a sophisticated sphere of human endeavour and necessity that people on their own can meet a community need with no assistance

[1] Professor B. C. Roberts, *Trade Unions in a Free Society*, 1959.
[2] *Not Unanimous—A Rival Verdict to Radcliffe's on Money*, edited by Arthur Seldon in 1969; and many other studies including Professor Friedman's *The Counter-Revolution in Monetary Theory*, 1970.
[3] Professor F. A. Hayek, *A Tiger by the Tail*, 1972.

from the state and entirely without state controls other than those designed to preserve the common law rights of individuals. To this end it is here proposed that an independent university be established for the provision of general higher education, the advancement of knowledge and the inculcation of habits of mental and moral discipline.'

Professor Ferns drew on the shortcomings of the state-financed universities to show the advantages of such radical departures as full-cost student fees backed by a loan scheme, a general education in humanities and sciences taken together with European languages, the encouragement of more mature students, and the ending of life tenure and of uniform pay scales for university teachers. To show that wide support for this radical proposal existed among leading educationists, the Paper by Professor Ferns included a declaration on 'The Urgency of the Independent University' which by the time the second edition was published in 1970 was signed by 100 university teachers and headmasters. Some readers no doubt thought the idea 'academic' in the sense of impractical. Yet within a year a Planning Board was set up under Sir Sydney Caine (a trustee of the IEA) and such progress was made that in 1973 it was succeeded by a fully-fledged Council for the University College of Buckingham. Having raised more than a million pounds, the Council hope to attract further benefactions[1] to enable the college to open for its first entry of students in 1975.

In the concluding paragraph of *Towards an Indepen-*

---

[1] Although fees will be fixed at a level to cover recurrent costs, the appeal is necessary to provide for scholarships and starting-up costs.

dent University, Professor Ferns clinched the case for this practical experiment in higher education by reference to a general proposition:

> 'If all knowledge is limited and uncertain, and all human beings and agencies make mistakes in their life strategy, the question is simply what arrangements will minimise the mistakes and maximise correct solutions.'

Professor Ferns and all those who have helped carry his idea towards practical achievement answer that question by their actions very much in the spirit of Hayek's definition of competition as 'the optimum discovery procedure'. If this new enterprise can demonstrate that students and teachers value the new freedoms of choice which it offers and which are not available in the increasingly 'homogenised' state-financed universities, it will not only be the student loan scheme which politicians and their reluctant civil service advisers may be pressed into adopting elsewhere.

More private research needed

Although I have frequently been told that there is no other organisation quite like the IEA, there are a number of groups in Britain and in America which have learned the advantage of putting their faith in scholarly research rather than political propaganda. On the other hand, there are a large and growing number of independent-looking research or educational bodies that are financed, partly or wholly and directly or indirectly, from public funds which must to some extent stop them from exposing all political prejudices to equal scrutiny and, where appropriate, equally uncompromising challenge. The fact that most economic 'research' throughout the world is done by government, or financed from public funds, makes it all the more vital to strengthen genuinely private study financed by a diversity of business sources and foundations which, as Sir Miles Clifford (of the Leverhulme Trust) argued in 1970, 'have more freedom to experiment, to share in adventure and search for new horizons than governments.'[1]

In 1850 a Mr Ellsworth, US Commissioner of Patents, was invited to discuss the building of a larger block of offices for the patents division. He counselled caution because he felt that just about everything that could be invented had already been invented. Up to the time Ellsworth expressed this opinion 3,327 patents had been taken out and since then a further 3,000,000 have been registered.

A similar episode occurred when General Grant, as President of the United States, was given the opportunity of talking over one of the first telephone lines. Having satisfied himself that the apparatus worked, he sat back and said: 'Yes, it is truly remarkable; but who in the world would ever want to use one of them?'

These may be amusing stories which indicate that the world has moved at a faster rate in the last hundred years or so than could have been foreseen. Yet had either Ellsworth or Grant possessed the power to decide what money would be spent on research and development, progress would have been stultified. So it is with economic research. My contention is that competition is just as much a discovery procedure in economics as in technical matters. The essential requirement is what Socrates called 'a private station',

[1] 'Needed: Fair Play for British Charity', *Reader's Digest*, October 1970.

in other words an independent base such as the IEA, which makes it possible to avoid political pressures and compromise.

I could say much more about the success of the educational strategy first suggested to me by Hayek in 1945. There have been difficulties, especially in financing the steady growth of this backroom activity (without taking public subsidies or becoming dependent on any other dominant source) and in warding-off people who wish to help, or sometimes to hinder,[1] by mixing the IEA up with party politics. But there has been no shortage of first-class authors or of subjects to which their analysis can be applied. Nor have they been content with scholarly criticism but have gone on to offer positive proposals about ways of extending competition among suppliers and choice among consumers. Some proof of this intellectual pudding is provided in my concluding chapter which outlines a programme drawing freely on what I have learned as a layman from IEA writers.

For reasons connected with the spread of political control and its accompanying high taxation, economists and others supporting the principle of reduced individual choice have had more 'research' funds at their disposal than independent intellectuals like Hayek, Mises or Popper, who have even so developed powerful arguments in favour of dispersed initiative and freedom of choice. I hope the examples I have given will encourage more people to study the neglected principle of maximising choice as the way to escape from the syndrome of disaster which has developed in the wake of its opposite. If the full strength of the argument for

[1] For example, by resorting to libellous words about the IEA, which on five occasions its legal advisers have required to be withdrawn.

choice has not yet come through what Hayek saw as the decisive intellectual debate, why should we expect legislation to move in that direction, except by chance?

As has been said of Christianity, the trouble with a policy to maximise choice in the modern world is not that it has been tried and failed, but that (with remarkable, perhaps temporary, exceptions like West Germany and Hong Kong) it has not yet been tried. It now provides perhaps the only hope of escape from more fashionable policies which have been tried and have failed utterly, again and again as we have seen.

CHAPTER 6

What Must be Done

A RADICAL PROGRAMME FOR ECONOMIC REFORM[1]

I have argued that the cause of the many social problems the world faces today, and has faced over many centuries, is lack of understanding of the natural laws or principles which govern human decision-making and human behaviour.

I have attempted to indicate the right principles, demonstrating that the vast fund of human good intentions too often produces unsatisfactory, even self-defeating consequences, but that an application of better understanding can remedy the situation. We have seen how good intentions lead politicians astray because their actions are based on confused assumptions and are confounded by party politics which are increasingly irrelevant and harmful. I have applied this thinking to historical events and modern developments which appear to confirm my diagnosis. Having studied the predictable dangers that arise from false principles, I have emphasised what I see to be the relationship between sound theory and its practical application by governments.

The final application of my thinking requires the

---

[1] This Chapter which sets out the policies that follow from my preceding argument owes much to the publications of the Institute of Economic Affairs and to discussions over many years with some of its authors. On the detailed figures for government expenditure and taxation, I was helped by an economist with extensive professional experience in such matters.

outline of an economic policy to implement it. This must be done without compromise, stating the objective and likely objections before setting down the programme for action. If my approach is right and sufficiently well-explained, this document will produce consequences through its effect on readers and reviewers who in turn will influence the politicians.

Grim prospect

I am writing with the conviction that there exists a distinctive positive policy to escape the clutches of a syndrome that appears to be leading towards increasing economic and political chaos on an international scale. On the negative side, unless such a change is made in national economic policy, we will stumble in ever more unpleasant spasms down the steep slope of economic ruin towards misery and dictatorship. History, for those who care to read, is full of gloomy and frightening precedents.

Standards of living have been rising because of technological progress in spite of political ineptitude. Politicians have survived, though only just, by claiming the credit but have increasingly been shown up as out of their depth.

What follows is an economic policy for prosperity. Although at first few may take heed, more will pay attention as things get worse. The aim is to achieve a transformation within a ten-year period but there is every reason to expect that, like the German miracle, a dramatic improvement will begin soon after the policy of freedom is launched. Guided by our principles we may be astonished to find how little government intervention will be needed and how quickly our position is improved.

The conditions under which any new government is

likely to find itself may be very grim indeed, including some, or all, of the following features:

1. a rapid decline in the value of the £;
2. punitive taxes that cut into savings as well as take-home pay;
3. increasing taxes on things we buy;
4. multiplying price and wage controls;
5. increasing import and financial controls;
6. rationing and consequent black markets;
7. judges and courts unable to cope with all the offenders;
8. industrial strife, strikes, 'rebellion';
9. growing threat of unemployment and trade stagnation;
10. political and economic weakness at home, leading to more troubles abroad;
11. an increasingly serious decline in the standard of living for more and more people.

It will be in the context of this vicious circle that the public will demand change. It is, of course, possible that the situation will be so bad that conventional politicians will claim more time and even try to delay an election. There may be demands for a coalition for 'national emergency measures'. Such a virtual dictatorship based on the discredited 'consensus' would simply prolong the agony and delay the necessary changes.

Scope for choice
As politicians become less sure of themselves, and less able to offer any alternative policy which has not already been discredited, many would wrongly welcome a coalition. The fashionable fear of not wishing to 'abdicate responsibilities to the free market' will

obstruct a move in the right direction. The international monetary crisis will reappear and 'world bankers' will be exposed as emperors without clothes.

The compass-bearing which guides my journey into the future is that, though the choice of each of us must be limited in certain specific directions, true wealth is created at the fastest rate possible under any given set of conditions when individual choice is deliberately maximised. It therefore becomes the duty of government 'to plan to maximise choice'. This compass-bearing will lead us to our destination, which I define as follows:

(a) the fastest possible rate of growth of wages and other incomes and therefore of the range of choice, *especially for poorer people*;

(b) arrangements to take care of the relatively few handicapped or incompetent individuals who are unable to fend for themselves, without obstructing the efforts of the most able on whom prosperity especially depends.

Low taxation and limited government expenditure are necessary for both these aims. I shall demonstrate that it is necessary and possible to drop income tax down to 15 pence in the £, end surtax and capital gains tax, and replace VAT by a simpler sales tax. In the crisis that is almost bound to come, many policies that have been thought 'politically impossible' will at last have a chance to prove their effectiveness.

Signs of decline

Ever since the last war, politicians have made the British people feel a nagging sense of failure. Our national self-confidence has been sapped, we feel our problems are beyond solution, and complain of our

lot in a way once thought the mark of less successful
nations. It is no use blaming our decline on the loss of
the Empire. Britain was made neither great nor rich by
the Empire. We led the world before we acquired most
of our colonies and it is a myth that we owed our wealth
to exploiting them: our success was based on trade and
enterprise on fair terms in all countries open to us,
British or foreign.

Wealth and power were in any case only part of the
foundation of our world influence, which rested also on
the quality of British public life and political behaviour.
Our decline can be measured in a number of ways.
Firstly, there is the reduction in individual freedom.
Secondly, we see the growth of group envy and
discontent, and the disappearance of respect for
individual self-reliance. Success which comes from
people's own efforts is resented while the idea of self-
help and individual responsibility is attacked as anti-
social by leading intellectuals. Thirdly, we appear
unable to keep up with similar nations in economic
growth. We are bottom of the league in the rate of
economic growth among the world's developed countries. Whereas before the last war Britain had the highest
standard of living in Europe, we have now been
overtaken by all the other European countries except
Austria, Finland, Spain, Portugal, Italy and Greece.
Although it is true that at present the margins are
mostly narrow, other countries are moving ahead
faster so that before long we will be among the poorer
European nations unless we make a fundamental
change of course.

These sad developments have gone along with our
changed attitude to the state. We once regarded
government as chiefly concerned with protecting

K

peace abroad and order at home. Now we have come to look to the state as our universal provider. This attitude can lead only to poverty and tyranny.

A RADICAL APPROACH
Ending government monopoly and control

The first aim of government must be 'to set the people free', as Churchill put it. A new government must make its first priority maximising choice by removing the worst monopolies of all—those organised by the state—and withdrawing from the Common Market. Changing legislation is a slow process but some restrictions can be removed quickly. As a start the nationalised industries must be exposed to competition by removing barriers to entry. We must end state monopoly in coal-mining, gas, electricity, postal services, transport and nuclear power. At the same time, radio, television and telephone services should be thrown open to competitive tender.

The buying and selling of all agricultural produce, currencies and metals, including gold, should be freed. The National Economic Development Office and all other government 'economic planning departments', under whatever name, should be wound up. The power of the Chancellor of the Exchequer over the Bank of England must be ended, along with control over interest rates, the printing of money, and the fluctuating foreign exchange rates.

A number of government departments will become redundant, and therefore a system of demobilising the civil service—similar to that for demobilising the armed forces at the end of the war—must be prepared. Golden handshakes would be a cheap price to pay for reducing wasteful public expenditure, freeing thousands of able men and women for productive employment and releasing millions of square feet of scarce office space in London and other large towns.

Exchange controls must be wound up. Before the last war exchange control was regarded as an interference with basic freedom and the mark of the totalitarian economy such as that organised by Dr Schacht for Hitler's Germany. Yet politicians of all parties now seem to regard it as part of the natural order. Since the war they have told us that the state of our balance of payments will not permit the free transfer of funds outside the sterling area. After 25 years it is clear the restrictive policies will never lead to a balance-of-payments position in which the complete removal of exchange controls will be judged safe.

All forms of direct control over prices and incomes must be ended. They are devices not for the cure of inflation but for its repression. There is no known case of success at any time in this country or in any other. The result is always and everywhere to produce distortions which add to the damage done by continued inflation. In putting up with price and incomes control we demonstrate doubly our feeble acceptance of the claims of over-powerful politicians. By their power to over-spend, and to create money for that purpose, politicians cause inflation; and by their power to impose price and income controls they fasten responsibility for the inflation on innocent private citizens.

Enforcing competition
There must be a phased reduction in tariffs and agricultural subsidies, perhaps over three years to give entrepreneurs time to adjust their expectations. The economy will then be growing and prices will be falling.

These trends can be allowed for in the first year's Budget which follows. The 'loss' factor created by government activity and spending will increasingly be replaced by profits.

Once competition has been encouraged throughout the economy, a de-nationalisation process will already have begun. It will be necessary to sell off government assets rapidly, even if some buyers make large profits in the early days. There will, at first, be a reluctance to take over the assets, but so necessary is it to get competition back at work for the benefit of the workers and consumers that it may pay to take a low bid or give away some assets.

Legislation is necessary to make trade unions subject to the law of contract as enforced by the independent courts. It is not necessary to blame trade unions for causing rises in prices because of wage demands which are in turn provoked by inflation. But although our decline stems mostly from our changed attitude to the state, organised labour has had a damaging influence on the economy and society by obstructing new methods, excluding non-members from well-paid jobs, and causing unemployment by pushing wages ahead of the resulting poor achievement in productivity. Labour and Conservative politicians have not only extended union power, but have renounced the right and duty to protect the general public (and union members) from its consequences. As part of its policy of extending choice, the state should use the power of law to protect its citizens from coercion or aggression by powerful private pressure groups. In the labour market we have permitted a lawless situation in which the state watches impotently while trade unions or local, unofficial bodies of workers reduce the choice of fellow citizens.

However, though the main part of the remedy in the labour market must be the development and enforcement of a legal code for collective bargaining, there is a link between the present impotence of the state in labour matters and its overblown authority elsewhere. The decay of belief in free enterprise as the power of government has increased leads us also to accept oppression by organised labour even though we do not like it. At the same time, social welfare benefits are given to strikers who are cushioned against responsibility for indiscipline. Hence we have for a generation suffered a strange mixture of state control spreading everywhere except into the labour market where we are periodically threatened with anarchy.

Choice and competition for welfare

We all want a system that will supply better medical care, education, housing and pensions, and I have argued the proposition that the best services are available where competition and choice are most free. The difficulty is not in arranging competing suppliers of these services, but in ensuring that the poor can enjoy a better minimum standard than at present.

Radical reform can start by allowing everyone paying enough income tax to contract out of the NHS and to receive a rebate on producing evidence of having taken out a private health insurance policy. Private insurance schemes like BUPA, PPP and Western Provident will grow rapidly and offer varying choices to meet family preferences. Where family incomes are inadequate, vouchers with appropriate values can be given to cover the cost of basic health insurance.

A similar system can be adopted for education, as expounded by Professor Milton Friedman, Professor E. G. West and Dr Rhodes Boyson, with vouchers being available for state or private schooling. For university students, repayable loans must replace grants.

Our attitude to the state is reflected most clearly in the general acceptance of the tax burdens it now piles on almost everyone. High taxation is often thought of as a method for redistributing wealth and incomes in favour of the poor. Redistribution masquerades as a means for social equality but rests on the political power of the majority of voters to pick the pockets of a tiny minority. In fact, as a way of helping 'the poor' the progressive taxation of 'the rich' is a very minor factor. Redistribution, in short, is not the reason total taxes are high. With government now taking over half of the national income, the heavy burden of taxation must be borne by the mass of citizens for the simple reason that there is no other source from which such massive sums can come.

A major cause of the state's high demands is the misuse of resources due to the losses suffered when money is spent outside the competitive arena, especially in the nationalisation of welfare. The result is the same as in other nationalised industries, an inferior product at excessive cost. Hence the compulsory 'welfare state' is an engine for the impoverishment of welfare, not for its enrichment. For the vast majority of people, released from the taxes necessary to support state welfare, the free market will provide better welfare; and for the few who cannot afford market prices, a selective tax-supported voucher system will ensure a choice of better services than the present universal system. The welfare state is the outstanding example of our readiness to accept the claim of the modern state to be a benefactor when in practice it is an instrument of tyranny and poverty. It is no coincidence that most modern and many ancient dictators have claimed to provide universal welfare services.

It is often objected that Britain's poor growth record of the past twenty-five years cannot be a consequence of the welfare state because the fast-growing nations of Western Europe have also developed state welfare systems. There are at least three answers to this misleading half-truth.

In the first place, let us take the two most successful economies. In Switzerland the welfare state is no more than a stunted growth and in Germany it is largely subordinate to the needs of a vigorous private enterprise system, which even the Social Democratic Party has had to accept as the price of winning an election. It is well-known in Italy, though less so of France and Belgium, that the taxation system (despite 'welfarism') still leaves ample incentives to men of enterprise. It is only in the Netherlands and Sweden that state welfare matches the dominant role it has in Britain.

Secondly, in the way growth is measured by politicians, it is not a sure test of economic success. What we want is not statistical, short-term growth, but growth on stable foundations. Of the European countries, only Germany and Switzerland can claim with confidence that their post-war growth rests on stable foundations.

Thirdly, the full consequences of welfare state policies in Europe have not had time to be judged. It is still too early to assume that penal taxation in Scandinavia and the Netherlands can continue without weakening long-term economic performance. It is significant that British politicians have recently begun to excuse our inflation by saying that much the same is happening in other countries—which are increasingly pursuing similar policies in public expenditure, state welfare and monetary policy.

Hence the case remains as strong as before that a programme to revitalise the British economy calls for a drastic reduction of governmental expenditure and taxation. In accordance with our principle, the changes must be of a fundamental character to produce the necessary results, and we must not be frightened by the cry of 'political impossibility'. This alibi is raised to direct debate away from the merits of a proposal where the proposal itself cannot be proved wrong. It assumes that fashionable beliefs, whether they are true or false, cannot be changed although those beliefs themselves were not always accepted. We have seen that the best way to ensure that new ideas are carried into effect is to work them out in detail and put them on the record so that they can be judged on their merits. All the more is this so in a nation which is failing and which will, therefore, have sooner or later to look urgently for new ideas that can bring a new lease of life.

A TEN-YEAR PROGRAMME

Although the changes need to be fundamental, they cannot all be made over-night. Time is needed for individuals and firms to adjust to them and for a steady development from one change to another. Yet the pace of reform should not be too slow or else the programme will lose momentum and the full advantages be lost. Hence I have aimed at a period of ten

years which is long enough for a radical programme of
reform to yield its benefits, and short enough to
maintain enthusiasm and determination. But though
the programme needs time, the decision to embark
upon it cannot wait. The sooner the proposed changes
can be announced, the quicker people will adjust
their own plans to the new situation. The government
will have to allow some flexibility to meet uncertainties
that cannot be foreseen but not to depart from the
essential principles of choice and competition on which
the programme is based.

Projected income and explanation
Table 3 presents ten-year projections from 1972–3 of
governmental expenditure and its share of the country's
Gross National Product (GNP). The projection of this
share is essential to the exercise, since the rates of
taxation that will be necessary to cover expenditure
depend upon it. In 1972–3 the GNP is estimated at
about £55,000 million. On Projection I this rises in
ten years to £73,000 million at present-day prices; on
Projection II, it rises to £82,100 million. After a period
of rapid inflation the use of constant prices is necessary
to enable projections to be made in real, not money,
terms.

The assumptions behind Projection I about the
rate of increase in real GNP are shown in footnote 1 to
Table 3. These are quite cautious estimates and
represent the minimum that should be expected over
the ten-year period. The low estimate for the early
years allows for the possibility that it will take some time
for the programme to yield its full result, and that the
ending of inflation will at first cause a slackening of
activity in some sectors which will offset increases

TABLE 3

PUBLIC EXPENDITURE AND GROSS NATIONAL PRODUCT
ALTERNATIVE 10-YEAR PROJECTIONS: 1972–3 to 1982–3
(£ million at 1972–3 prices)

Financial Year	Government Expenditure	Projection I[1] GNP	%	Projection II[2] GNP	%
1972–73	27,900	55,000	51	55,000	51
1973–74	28,500	56,000	51	56,000	51
1974–75	26,500	57,400	46	57,700	46
1975–76	24,300	58,800	41	59,400	41
1976–77	22,200	60,300	37	61,200	33
1977–78	20,300	62,100	33	64,300	31
1978–79	18,500	64,000	29	67,500	27
1979–80	17,800	65,900	27	70,900	25
1980–81	16,700	68,200	24	74,500	22
1981–82	15,600	70,600	22	78,200	20
1982–83	14,500	73,000	20	82,100	18

[1] *Projection I* assumes GNP rises at 2% p.a. from 1972–3 to 1973–4, 2½% p.a. to 1976–7, 3% p.a. to 1979–80, and 3½% p.a. to 1982–3.

[2] *Projection II* assumes GNP rises at 2% p.a. from 1972–3 to 1973–4, 3% p.a. to 1976–7, and 5% p.a. to 1982–3.

Sources: Public Expenditure to 1976–77, Cmnd. 5178, HMSO.
National Income and Expenditure, 1973, HMSO.
Monthly Digest of Statistics, HMSO.

elsewhere. Thereafter, the increases from $2\frac{1}{2}$ to $3\frac{1}{2}$ per cent are easily attainable, and are well below those achieved in Western Europe in the past 20 years. On these modest estimates GNP would rise by nearly 33 per cent in real terms over ten years.

The alternative assumptions behind Projection II would produce a rise of about 50 per cent in GNP over the ten years.

Projection II is certainly not over-optimistic, and may err on the side of caution. After all, one of the

most powerful clogs on economic progress—apart from
government—is the overmanning of industry. By North
American standards we employ in manufacturing,
mining and transport two men where one would
suffice; by German and Swiss standards, even allowing
for the use there of less-skilled Mediterranean labour,
we employ five or more in manufacturing where four
would suffice. It is not too much to expect that on
present techniques we succeed in reducing manning in
manufacturing, mining and transport by 25 per cent
and in distribution by 5 per cent, while 'output' in
central and local government service is reduced by
50 per cent. Even if we assume that other occupations
show no improvement, the result would still be an
increase in GNP of about 18 per cent even without
further technical progress, improvement in knowledge,
or expansion of investment. On this basis an increase
in GNP of 50 per cent in ten years becomes a modest
aim. Such improvements in manning are well within
reach and could be achieved almost immediately if the
anarchy in our system of collective bargaining were
ended. The reduction in government 'output' would
follow naturally from the operation of a programme to
reduce public expenditure by 50 per cent. In the light
of these considerations, it is reasonable to take Projection II as a sound, even cautious, basis for taxation
proposals. Even if we did no better than raise total
output according to the lower target of Projection I, we
could reduce taxes on a scale that would today appear
to the majority of taxpayers to be quite impossible. It
must be understood that a British government could
not carry out many of the changes I am proposing
unless it is freed from the restrictions imposed by our
membership of the EEC.

Cutting government spending

Table 4 shows the proposed reduction of public expenditure by almost 50 per cent in real terms over the ten-year period under its main heads. The figures for any given year after 1972–3 are of course rough estimates which convey an idea of the tempo of economies rather than the precise result for any given year up to 1982–3 when the stated target could certainly be achieved.

Health services. At present Britain spends less per head on all forms of medical care than most other comparable countries, but the shortfall in value for money is almost certainly more than the shortfall in the money spent (wastefully) under the bureaucratic NHS. Socialised medicine has thus proved to be a serious brake on the development of health services. Our aim should be a system in which, ultimately, the only state responsibilities are for public health (i.e. prevention of epidemics, inspection of abattoirs, restaurant kitchens, etc.), aid for the very poor (especially the aged) in paying for health, and the care of long-term mental hospital inmates. All other health provision should be privately financed (mainly, of course, through insurance). The figures in Table 4 reflect this aim. They start from the present level, since the reform of the socialised system must take some time even to introduce, and then fall gradually over nine years by almost three-quarters to £800 million in present-day money.

Education. Present policy is based on the once-fashionable belief that all education must be a good thing; that expenditure on education therefore yields high dividends, especially in the form of economic growth; and that the public educational budget must accordingly

TABLE 4

TOTAL PUBLIC EXPENDITURE
10-YEAR PROJECTION: 1972-3 to 1982-3
(£ million at 1972-3 prices)

	1972-3	1973-4	1974-5	1975-6	1976-7	1977-8	1978-9	1979-80	1980-1	1981-2	1982-3
Defence	3,000	3,200	3,400	3,400	3,400	3,400	3,400	3,400	3,400	3,400	3,400
Health and personal social services	2,900	2,800	2,400	2,100	1,700	1,400	1,100	1,000	900	800	800
Education	3,550	3,500	3,100	2,900	2,600	2,300	2,000	2,000	2,000	2,000	2,000
Housing	1,400	1,300	1,100	800	600	500	400	350	250	200	150
Retirement pensions	2,350	2,450	2,500	2,400	2,300	2,300	2,100	2,000	1,900	1,900	1,900
Unemployment	250	250	250	250	250	250	250	250	250	250	250
Sickness and industrial injuries	500	450	400	300	250	200	200	200	200	200	250
Other social security	1,950	1,900	1,800	1,450	1,450	1,250	1,250	1,200	1,100	900	800
Industrial subsidies, grants, etc.	2,250	2,100	1,750	1,450	1,200	1,050	850	650	550	550	450
Roads	1,000	1,100	1,100	1,100	1,000	900	900	900	700	700	700
Nationalised industries (capital)	1,800	1,750	1,600	1,350	1,150	850	650	550	400	300	0
Overseas aid, EEC and other overseas services	500	500	400	300	200	200	200	200	150	150	150
Administration and non-specified items	4,100	4,500	4,100	4,000	3,800	3,700	3,200	3,200	3,000	2,350	1,800
Debt interest	2,350	2,700	2,600	2,500	2,300	2,000	2,000	1,900	1,900	1,900	1,900
TOTAL	27,900	28,500	26,500	24,300	22,200	20,300	18,500	17,800	16,700	15,600	14,500

Source: Public Expenditure to 1976-77, Cmnd. 5178, HMSO.

be expanded indefinitely. Under the influence of these
ideas educational expenditure has risen faster than any
other major element in the state's budget, and would
anyway produce unmanageable financial problems
unless the trend of policy is soon reversed.

If we examine fashionable beliefs we will find that it
is not true that *any* kind of education has merit; nor is
it true that all expenditure on education necessarily
produces high dividends, whether in economic growth
or otherwise; nor is it true that such expansion in
educational expenditure as is desirable must be
financed by government. Present policies are bound to
lead to waste and dissatisfaction on a massive scale.

The aims of radical reform should be complete
independence for universities, with state expenditure
confined to services (e.g. research) purchased by the
state and scholarships for outstanding scholars; private
payment of fees assisted by loans for all higher education; and partial payment assisted by vouchers for
primary and junior secondary schooling. On this basis
the public educational budget could be brought down
in ten years to an approximate figure of £2,000 million
from the present £3,550 million. Such a programme
would not merely reduce the governmental budget for
education, but would improve the whole educational
system by exposing the school and university bureaucracy to experiment and innovation. In education, as
elsewhere, competition can work as a discovery
procedure.

In the process, some forms of education would no
doubt be cut down. Among these would probably be
university education, which many people think has
been over-expanded in the post-war years. Until
potential students can choose whether or not to go to

university in the light of the cost—and of the alternative ways of spending the money—there is no reason for thinking all the present places are worth paying for.

Housing. Recent policies combine the maximum of waste and unfairness. Rent controls have all but destroyed the private market in rented accommodation and have caused the decay of millions of houses which otherwise would have been well maintained. At the same time, public funds have been invested on an enormous scale in council houses to take the place of private provision. There is no necessity for government to provide housing, apart from some very exceptional cases connected with slum clearance. If a tenant's income falls below a tolerable level, it is his income not his rent that should be subsidised, and this should be done from the national assistance budget ('supplementary benefits') without destroying the free market in rented housing. In our Projection expenditure on public housing is therefore reduced from £1,400 million to £150 million by the end of ten years.

Pensions. An especially bad feature of the welfare state is the pauperisation of a substantial proportion of the aged. Inflation and high taxation have prevented them from making adequate retirement provision for themselves, and they are left the helpless dependants of the state. Their needs burden the budget as politicians bid for their votes by promising higher pensions for the needy and non-needy alike. The solution here as elsewhere is the extension of private provision. But the long-term nature of state pensions means that their cost cannot be sharply reduced within the short period of ten years. First, the proportion of the population of pension age is growing. Secondly, the only tolerable

way to get state pensions out of our system is to continue
to pay them to existing pensioners and to scale them
down year by year for a period of, say, 25–30 years.

Thus we might decide that persons aged 64 would
get the full pension next year; persons aged 63 would
get the full pension less 1/25 or 1/30; persons aged 62
would get the full pension less 2/25 or 2/30, and so on.
In this way on a 25-year scale, no one now under the
age of 39 would get a state pension at all. For the
balance, each employed person would be required to
take out a minimum policy, paying the premium out
of the reduction in personal taxation and choosing
from a variety of competitive schemes. Such a system
would take a considerable time to produce a substantial
reduction in state expenditure. Hence the figure in our
Projection for 1982–3 is not very much less than that
for 1972–3, and for the early years the figures actually
show a rise as the number of pensioners increases.
However, the cost would go on falling after 1982–3,
thereby providing a margin for other expenditure if
the budget was maintained at about £14,500 million
at 1972–3 prices.

Unemployment. On the assumption that unemployment
would be held roughly steady over the ten-year period,
the 1972–3 figure is adopted for the rest of the period.
The 1972–3 figure allows for payments to many who
are not genuinely unemployed, but the continued
provision of £250 million allows for improvement in
benefits to the genuinely unemployed in future. The
amount is so small compared with the total budget that
even a sizeable error would not have a significant
effect on it.

Defence. No one can know with certainty the future

requirements of defence expenditure, for it will be determined by influences largely outside our control. We work only on the basis of rough general considerations. The safest reckoning might be that defence is the one main heading of expenditure which in real terms should *not* be reduced. Decisions to reduce defence expenditure can be based only on the hope that no one will attack us or our interests or that others will defend us. There are no rational grounds for such a hope, although short-sighted politicians are always tempted to close their eyes to distant dangers of the world as a pretext for spending lavishly on their pet projects. Furthermore, since weapons are certain to become more complicated and expensive, *effective* defence is likely to cost more and ineffective defence is not worth paying for anyway. Hence it would seem sensible to allow for an increase in expenditure in real terms over the ten years, and the figures in Table 4 accordingly show a rise from £3,000 million to £3,400 million from 1972-3 to 1974-5 after which they are held constant.

In singling out defence as the one main heading under which expenditure should not fall, I must emphasise that all these figures refer to governmental spending only. Thus drastic reductions in *public* spending on health, education, housing, pensions do not mean that *total* expenditure on these services should fall. On the contrary the prosperity of an efficient competitive economy would leave individuals free to spend more, and probably much more, on these purposes than is now spent for them by governments out of taxation. But the proportion of private expenditure would rise and that of public expenditure would fall. Defence is a special case since the whole of the expenditure must be undertaken by governments.

L

Sickness and industrial injuries. The abuse of sickness benefit is now a national scandal. The cost is running at over £500 million, is rising fast, and can be cut down sharply. At 1972–3 prices the figure should not exceed £200 million in 1982–3. Industrial injury benefit which at present amounts to over £100 million ought to be taken out of the state system and returned to voluntary insurance.

Other social security. The main items here are supplementary benefits, widows' pensions, and child allowances. For some years supplementary benefits may have to be increased in certain directions. The reason is that in emancipating the people from the shams of the welfare state, we shall find it necessary to provide more generous aid for the exceptionally needy. On the other hand there is a slackness in the administration of these benefits as there is with sickness benefit. Hence on balance it is probable that the net amount could be reduced gradually but substantially. Widows' pensions would continue but, like supplementary benefits, subject to needs tests; and in a thriving free economy with low taxation and rising real incomes universal child allowances would have no justification.

Industrial subsidies, grants, etc. These would have no place in a healthy and advancing free economy in which the test of business success is making profit and avoiding loss, and in which profit like other forms of incomes would be lightly taxed. They ought therefore to be completely abolished, but a smallish figure of £450 million is left in the Projection for 1982–3 in case abolition cannot be completed over ten years: subsidies on a small scale to hill farmers, for example, and research grants might take a considerable time to phase out. The 1972–3 figure of £2,250 million includes over £300 million for investment grants. The reduction of company and other taxation would enable them to be completely abolished.

Roads. Here the Projection assumes that expenditure must initially rise. The government is in process of constructing a nation-wide motorway system which must rise in cost in the near future. Thereafter the cost of the road system (motor, country and urban) must remain substantial. However, the figure ought to fall after a few years, both because the motorway system will be nearing completion and because costs can be partially recouped by tolls on the motorways and by new methods of charging for the use of urban road space.

Investment by nationalised industries. Over the ten-year period this item can be completely abolished since all nationalised industries can by then be returned to private hands. It is another myth that a private capital market cannot develop for the purchase of these industries, especially for the two great loss-makers of coal and the railways. All property can be disposed of at some price, and it would even pay the nation to sell off the coal and railway industries at bargain prices. A resounding success is necessary during these ten years to let all politicians see that the experiment with nationalisation is over and cannot be repeated.

The Post Office. This monopoly service costs nearly £600 million a year for capital investment and is an outstanding candidate for early denationalisation. This would leave private enterprise to finance its future developments from the ordinary capital market.

Overseas aid, etc. The amount involved here may not seem very large but is rising. Most overseas 'aid' is unproductive, may have opposite results from those intended, and ought to be ended. Much other expenditure in this category arises from the excessive growth of governmental functions at home (e.g. the excessive expansion of personnel at embassies) and from membership of the EEC. The result of our Projection is to reduce the figure to £150 million.

Administration, etc. This very large group (£4,100 million approximately in 1972–3) includes many items which reflect essential governmental duties and which may require increased expenditure (e.g. police, the judiciary, the prison system, factory inspection, shipping and inland transport regulations). But administration is the largest element, especially in local government where the bureaucracy has been increased in recent years without concern for economy or efficiency. Hence, immense savings can be made by reducing the functions of government as already indicated in this programme. The 1972–3 figure can comfortably be reduced over the ten years to an amount in the region of £1,800 million.

Debt interest. Central and local government debt interest now amounts annually to about £2,350 million. It is most unlikely to be capable of reduction at all for some years, and even over the whole period of ten years it will not be possible to reduce it by a large amount. For the period we are concerned with the amount of debt interest will be largely influenced by three factors.

In the first place, as the programme proceeds, private

saving is certain to rise. Rates of interest are then likely to fall but it is unlikely that during the next ten years they will fall to the levels of the mid-fifties. There is thus little chance of reducing interest on long-term debt by funding during the term of the programme. But there should be savings in short-term debt interest.

Secondly, as denationalisation goes ahead, together with a general reduction in government expenditure, the borrowing requirements of central and local authorities will fall sharply. And thirdly, rates of interest have recently risen to exceptionally high levels and are unlikely to fall dramatically until fears of inflation are finally laid to rest. Hence it is best to assume that interest on maturing debt which is refunded in the near and medium term must be high.

Taking into account these factors, which partly balance out, the Projection assumes a rise in debt interest up to 1973–4 and thereafter a slow decline to about £1,900 million.

HOW TAXES WILL COME DOWN

We can now consider how our projected figures for government expenditure can be translated into possible reductions in taxation. In round figures the total in 1972–3 was estimated at £27,900 million, whereas taxation was estimated at £22,000 million. The difference is made up by non-tax income (rents, interest, and trading surpluses of government agencies and local authorities) plus borrowing. Since the purpose of my programme is to get government out of business, we must expect that this non-tax income will disappear, apart from small local authority trading surpluses and some residual rents and interest. We also assume that there will be no net governmental long-term borrowing at the end of the term of the programme. On this basis, total taxation could be reduced over the ten years from £22,000 million at 1972–3 prices to £13,500 million, or by nearly 40 per cent.

There are many ways in which this total reduction can be converted into reduced rates of particular taxes. Some taxes may be abolished or reduced more than others. New and less damaging taxes may be devised in their place. For example, some form of reverse income tax could reduce taxation still further if it is used to replace most other forms of state benefits in cash and kind. Furthermore, the changes in rates of tax, as distinct from the total of taxation, will depend upon the rate of increase achieved in GNP. For example, a rise in GNP by 50 per cent combined with a fall in taxation by 40 per cent would enable average tax rates to fall by more than 60 per cent.

There is clearly no single best way of deciding which taxes to reduce or increase and by how much. There are arguments for specially reducing taxes on incomes to encourage incentives, and for cutting taxes on goods and services to avoid distorting competition and choice. However, whichever view we may take on particular taxes, the three principles which should guide the reforms are simplicity, equity and efficiency. Above all, efficiency means we should remove as far as possible tax discouragements to effort, enterprise, economy and saving.

In the light of these principles and of the estimates for total governmental expenditure and of Projection II for GNP, the following is the kind of streamlined tax structure that could replace the present incomprehensible muddle ten years from now.

A. *Taxes on Income*

1. *Income Tax:* a uniform rate of 15 per cent with allowances which would exempt a single person from tax at an income of £800 p.a., a married man at £1,300, and a married man with two children at £1,700. There would be no going back to an 'earned' income allowance and the life insurance allowance would be abolished. The surcharge on investment income would be abolished.

2. *Corporation Tax:* at the income tax rate of 15 per cent in the £ with a credit against the shareholder's personal tax of the tax paid on his dividends.

B. *Taxes on Capital*

1. *Estate Duty:* a flat rate of 20 per cent above a £25,000 exemption level. The present rules of survivorship whereby gifts before death are taxed at death would be abolished; but a gifts tax at the same rate of estate duty would be imposed on gifts, with annual exemptions and a £25,000 lifetime exemption.

2. *Capital Gains Tax:* abolished.

C. *Taxes on Expenditure*

1. *Alcohol and tobacco:* rates reduced by 25 per cent.

2. *Motor fuel and motor vehicle licences:* rates reduced by 40 per cent.

3. *Fuel oil:* abolished.

4. *VAT:* replaced by a retail sales tax (see below).

5. *Customs duties:* reduced to negligible proportions.

6. *Betting duties:* continued at present rates.

7. *Stamp duties:* abolished.
8. *Sales tax:* levied at 5 per cent on all sales to consumers, including services, but not food. Although the sales tax is considerably more costly to administer than purchase tax (over which it has compensating advantages), it is far simpler to understand and administer than VAT which Britain was required to adopt as a member of EEC.

D. National Insurance Contributions

Reduced to cover unemployment and sickness benefit only; since pensions and general relief would be met out of general revenue, the rates of contribution would be reduced by about 85 per cent.

E. Local Rates

Poundage reduced by about 60 per cent on average.

Even if we adopted the pessimistic assumptions for the GNP of Projection I, the rates of tax by 1982–3 would fall to levels which would appear beyond the dreams of the great majority of our citizens, with income tax and corporation tax at 20 per cent and reductions in excise duties of 20–30 per cent and local rates halved.

It will be a revelation to most people that these calculations are possible. The analysis has history and logic to support it, and the calculations have been thoroughly checked against official figures. It is my contention that as soon as a few leaders grasp the arguments and the consequences, they will arouse the public to demand that economic measures along these lines are put into effect.

A LAST WORD

For some busy people into whose hands my book falls, this conclusion may be all that is read. The old Negro preacher used to say:

> 'First, I tells 'em what I'm gonna tell 'em; then I tells 'em; and finally I tells 'em what I told 'em.'

Likewise, I have hammered away at my basic belief that the history of economic troubles repeats itself and does so not by chance or bad intentions but because some law of human behaviour is not understood or applied.

Not bad men . . .

A recurring syndrome in history is that after a period of relative prosperity inflation develops, government takes more power away from individual consumers and producers, taxes increase, every failure of control leads to a further spread of bureaucracy, the value of money goes on dropping until the government resorts to some variant of wages and prices policy. Since such freezes or squeezes cause further pain without curing the original disease, they provoke even more serious political disorder.

Leaving aside the alibi of bad luck, and recalling that in Europe, as well as more recently in Asia and Africa, this recurring sequence has often concluded with a dictator who minimises the choice of the individual almost to zero, the explanation could be that history periodically throws up people with evil intentions who enslave their fellow human beings in the guise of acting 'in the interests of the people and

151

for the benefit of the working man'. But seeing today in Britain how well-intentioned politicians are heading the same disastrous way, I discount the possibility that bad men can generally be blamed for the syndrome repeating itself.

. . . but ignorance

So I conclude that the root of our troubles is the failure to understand logical cause-and-effect relationships. The distilled wisdom of the ages, which comes down from Socrates and other philosophers, has been expressed in the following aphorism.

> 'He who knows not, and knows not that he knows not, is a fool; shun him. But he who knows not, and knows that he knows not, is wise; follow him.'

I have come to the conclusion that the syndrome repeats itself because human beings act in ignorance and therefore in unconscious defiance of certain natural laws and principles.

If human beings are to convert good intentions into good results they have to study cause-and-effect relationships in economics—as has only relatively recently in man's history been done in the natural sciences. But in matters governing human relationships there is disagreement whether true principles apply. Laws are made by government but, if no consistent cause-and-effect relationship exists, the outcome will not be as intended. I have provided abundant evidence that there is confusion on this subject and that, as an ordinary citizen faced with the consequences of bad government, I am entitled to say that many if not most 'experts' have been proved wrong.

From principles to practice

In my attempt as a non-economist to define a possible fundamental principle, I have suggested that 'wealth is created at the fastest possible rate when individual choice is deliberately maximised.' Under such conditions the incomes and choices of the poorest will increase most rapidly. The reverse of this principle seems to explain the failure of authoritarian governments, like the communists, which reduce choice and retard improvements in standards of living for the masses. It is necessary to emphasise that 'choice-maximised' is not what is generally understood to be 'permissiveness'. It does not mean that everyone can do as they please. It means that government is required to establish laws which maximise individual choice. A contemporary example is the double white line down the middle of a dangerous road which confines each driver to one-half of the road, but maximises everybody's choice by facilitating fuller and safer use of the public highway.

If there is a sound economic principle, how can we ensure it will be applied? I have tried to explain from history that, to be effective, well-founded understanding must be documented. This is an arduous exercise which is widely under-rated because 'thinking' is regarded as less effective than 'action'. Well-intentioned people almost invariably turn to party politics, lobbying or demonstrations, which are too often forms of action without thinking and so lead to the syndrome of failure and ultimately disillusionment.

There are many whose occupation is thinking. But these are mostly either 'academics' who are often financed by governments and so influenced by prevailing ideas of what is thought 'politically possible', or

politicians and civil servants who are responsible for
the policies that have failed. It is unlikely that economists dependent on this establishment will uncom-
promisingly expose its failure and point to a quite
different way ahead.

It can be done—again

From my study of history I contend that there is
abundant evidence that the syndrome has repeated
itself because of a general failure to understand that an
unpleasant situation will be made worse by policies
that reduce individual choice. Thus at its simplest,
more controls and more taxes are applied in an attempt
to undo the evils created by too much control and
taxes. In contrast, there have been examples through
the ages when governments have maximised choice
instead of minimising it, and prosperity has followed,
sometimes on an almost miraculous scale.

I have studied some recent events which suggest that
'choice-maximised' has produced prosperity and
'choice-minimised' the syndrome. I have speculated
that we can equate the benefits of 'choice-maximised'
with profits and the hardships of 'choice-minimised'
with losses. As a rough guide, we can expect that when
government expenditure reaches about half of the
gross national product, 'losses' may cancel out benefits
and national growth will consequently slow down to
zero. The measurement of voluntary as opposed to
involuntary exchanges is not easy but it is apparent
that inflation and high government expenditure go
together and both erode free choice.

Having provided some encouraging examples of the
power of understanding when it is clearly documented, my final Chapter applies the lesson by setting

out a detailed programme that would dramatically reduce government spending and put Britain back on the road to economic recovery and general wellbeing. Many, I am sure, will welcome my approach but may wonder if it disregards what is, often quite wrongly, thought to be 'politically impossible'. I invite each reader to study my case and make up his mind, independently of preconceptions, whether it is soundly based on correct principles.